THE
RIP

THE RIP

True Stories of Stock Brokerage Corruption

BRET AITA

Published by ECW PRESS
2120 Queen Street East, Suite 200, Toronto, Ontario, Canada M4E 1E2

NATIONAL LIBRARY OF CANADA CATALOGUING IN PUBLICATION DATA
Aita, Bret
The rip: true stories of stock brokerage corruption / Bret Aita.
ISBN 1-55022-570-7
1. Stockbrokers—Malpractice—Case studies. I. Title.

HG4928.5.A37 2003   364.16'8   C2002-905434-6

Acquisition Editor: Robert Lecker
Copy Editor: Mary Williams
Cover design: David Drummond
Interior design: Guylaine Régimbald—Solo Design
Typesetting: Yolande Martel
Production: Emma McKay
Printing: Transcontinental

This book is set in Bulmer and Trade Gothic

The publication of *The Rip: True Stories of Stock Brokerage Corruption* has
been generously supported by the Canada Council, by the Government of
Ontario through the Ontario Media Development Corporation's Ontario Book
Initiative, by the Ontario Arts Council, and by the Government of Canada
through the Book Publishing Industry Development Program. Canadä

DISTRIBUTION

CANADA: Jaguar Book Group, 100 Armstrong Avenue,
Georgetown, Ontario L7G 5S4

UNITED STATES: Independent Publishers Group, 814 North Franklin Street,
Chicago, Illinois 60610

EUROPE: Turnaround Publisher Services, Unit 3, Olympia Trading Estate,
Coburg Road, Wood Green, London N2Z 6T2

AUSTRALIA AND NEW ZEALAND: Wakefield Press, 1 The Parade West
(Box 2266), Kent Town, South Australia 5071

PRINTED AND BOUND IN CANADA

ECW PRESS
ecwpress.com

Contents

Introduction

Who can forget the maniacal character Gordon Gekko from the 1987 movie *Wall Street*? His attitude towards business was chillingly callous, and he summed it up like this: "Greed . . . is good. Greed is right. Greed works."

While the concept of corporate America as an evil empire isn't exactly new, during the past 15 years it's been more relevant than ever. Recently, the investing public has been given a graphic demonstration of just how pervasive corruption and greed have become in the American business world.

The decade of the 1990s was a golden age of economic prosperity for many Americans. Even habitually conservative investors were swept up in the rush to turn huge market profits. And when everyone is raking it in, no one asks too many questions. No one wants to rock the boat. But when the bubble finally burst, in March 2000, investors who had lost their shirts focused in on the overvaluation of many listed companies and the outrageous salaries of their CEOs. They were left with a bad taste in their mouths—things didn't seem quite as fair as they had when the markets were surging.

During that prolonged surge, investors had felt warmly towards their brokers, and in this environment of trust, the unscrupulous did not hesitate to exploit the gullible. While his excited clients "played the markets" and watched their investments multiply, a devious broker could easily sneak in a scam stock with a basket of securities containing market leaders such as Microsoft or Intel, or push an overvalued (many times worthless) penny stock representing some new "technological breakthrough." He could bet that few would want to miss out on a "ground-floor opportunity" or a "volume play."

Of course, corrupt practices such as these could not escape the watchful eyes of the industry regulators. Many unethical and criminal brokers and dealers—even those against whom no investor complaints had been filed—found themselves slapped with fines, barred from working in the industry, or sent to prison. Cameron Funkhouser, vice president of market regulation for the National Association of Securities Dealers (NASD—a leading provider of market regulatory services), estimated that only about 1 percent of the industry's brokers and dealers were corrupt. But he also noted that even such a small faction could shatter investor confidence and do severe damage to the industry.

This rogue 1 percent stole billions from investors during the 1990s, using all kinds of fraudulent and manipulative strategies. Many squandered their illicit gains on drugs, prostitutes, gambling, and wild parties. They developed a culture of decadence and excess, reveling in the high life. Few probably ever gave a thought to the fact that the practice on which they'd built their lavish lifestyle—securities fraud—has a long history.

As early as 1285, the city of London, England required stockbrokers to hold licenses. By the late 1600s, the British Parliament had instituted regulations concerning traded offerings. In 1834, a couple of French bankers were caught paying off telegraph operators to disseminate false information about certain stocks, and their plot to artificially inflate the prices of these stocks, which they of course held, was foiled.

In the post–World War I prosperity of the 1920s, federal regulation of the U.S. securities industry was almost nonexistent. An estimated 20 million investors entered the markets during this time, all hoping to hit it big. Due to the lack of market regulation, unethical businesspeople were able to introduce fraudulent companies and misrepresent the value of their offerings. The Securities and Exchange Commission (SEC) estimates that in the course of the decade, $50 billion in newly issued stock flooded the market. A staggering 50 percent turned out to be worthless by the time overspeculation led to the infamous crash of October 1929. Shell-shocked investors ran to their banks and withdrew all of their savings, causing a cash crisis and triggering a full-scale economic depression.

But after World War II the economy once again began to thrive, and the industrial complex of the United States started to take shape. As the economy grew, so did the markets, and by the 1980s the U.S. economy had emerged as the undisputed champion in the global economic ring. Supported by the rise of capitalism, Reaganomics, and the federal government's laissez-faire attitude towards big business, resourceful businessmen began developing aggressive campaigns to make huge amounts of money. Among the most notorious of this bold new class of entrepreneur was a first-generation Russian-American named Ivan Boesky.

Boesky amassed his multimillion-dollar fortune by buying up shares of companies targeted for takeover by larger corporations. He identified these targets by manipulating an extensive network of contacts: directors and officers of companies, high-powered brokers, and knowledgeable insiders. It is strictly illegal to buy and sell securities based on information that is not available to the public. It's called insider trading. In 1986, the SEC levied a $100-million fine against Boesky for insider trading. Boesky was sent to prison the same year. He was released in 1990. During his prison term, he'd maintained a net worth of nearly $100 million.

One of Boesky's most prominent tipsters was Michael Milken, the control person of the country's fifth-largest brokerage firm—Drexel Burnham Lambert. Milken traded on that information himself, building a personal fortune of nearly two billion dollars. As part of a plea bargain, Boesky handed his ace tipster over to the authorities, and Milken was charged with over 90 counts of insider trading and racketeering. However, most of these charges were dropped when Milken did a little plea bargaining of his own and agreed to pay a fine of $650 million. He was ultimately sentenced to 10 years in prison, but he still managed to retain over one billion in cash and assets.

It was during this era that the term "boiler room" was coined. In the brokerage industry, the boiler room is the trading floor where legions of brokers ply their trade in an atmosphere of intense pressure and frenetic activity. And in boiler rooms nationwide, the face of the financial industry was changing dramatically. Suddenly, the stodgy, conservative broker in the gray three-piece suit was a dinosaur, forced into extinction by the fast-talking wiseguy.

In that pressure-cooker environment, the weak didn't last long, and this gave rise to a new breed of stockbroker. He was the kind of player who was short on knowledge and experience, but at that point stocks were so overvalued that you could throw five at the wall and three would stick. What he possessed was the ability to push securities to the seemingly insatiable investing public at a relentless rate.

By the time the 1990s hit and the markets entered the dot-com bubble, there were few obstacles confronting those who wanted to participate in the profession. If you wanted to sling stock and set up deals for a living, all you needed was a knack for selling. The profession harbored high school dropouts, graduate-degree holders, and everyone in between. If you could pass the ominous Series 7 licensing exam, handle 12 to 16 hours daily of cold calling, and resign yourself to receiving a salary of $500 a month (usually a draw against future commissions), then you could have a shot at being a stockbroker and making some serious money.

And there was some very serious money to be made. Typically, a successful boiler-room broker of the 1990s pulled in anywhere from $20,000 to $40,000 per month. It's true that not many survived the pressure cooker long enough to make this kind of cash, but those who did lived like kings and queens.

Salespeople know that three things stimulate the consumer to buy: sex, greed, and fear. In the 1990s, greed ruled. And the greediest of all were the brokers themselves. Many of the boiler-room brokers came from modest beginnings. For the first time in their lives, they found themselves in possession of large amounts of money, and, as I mentioned earlier, they cut loose.

In the boutique brokerages that had sprung up across the

country, many chop-shop stock jockeys used drugs to ease the pressure or to celebrate their financial coups. Cocaine was the drug of choice, but Ecstasy, crystal meth, and marijuana also abounded. Heavy drinking was another aspect of this party culture, which in some ways resembled that of the college fraternity. Brash young brokers would also let off steam by congregating in strip clubs, or "peeler joints." Some would hire prostitutes or escorts. It was fairly common to see strippers employed as sales assistants or receptionists strutting around in the boiler rooms. Gambling was another favorite stock-jockey pastime. Las Vegas, Atlantic City, or any town with a racetrack attracted them in droves. Tales of what went on during these decadent retreats became legendary among those who aspired to join the ranks of the successful, inspiring them to push harder—after all, only those who could withstand the pressure could afford such lavish indulgences.

It is important to note that although the stockbrokers themselves were the contact points for most investors during this era, they were not usually in charge of the operation. A handful of control people would set up the deals that the brokers pitched. They were the principals of the brokerage firms, company insiders, or brokers who had been in the business long enough to realize that the real money—the millions versus the thousands of dollars—was in deal making.

Most of the time, members of the frontline sales force were oblivious to what they were selling. They were the foot soldiers of the control people, and they were kept in the dark as to the structure of the various deals. The control people were usually the ones most deeply involved in any criminal activity. They had the intelligence and the malevolence to orchestrate and implement the investor rip-off schemes. Their scams ranged from the classic "pump and dump" to more complex short-selling undertakings, and they used various legal mechanisms—such as shell companies, reverse mergers, and Internet ventures—to carry out their illicit operations.

"The rip" is the term used to describe the per-share kick-back that the control people use to motivate their stockbrokers. As you read this book, you'll get a glimpse into the lifestyle of the boiler-room brokers, and you'll learn about some of the fraud structures employed by securities scam artists. The lifestyle stories are told in a series of exposés derived from firsthand experience and interviews with a number of boiler-room stock-brokers. The chapters that explore how the scams work contain examples taken from the case files of the SEC and the NASD. My intention here is to provide you, the reader, with a detailed understanding of how investors' money was stolen and how a lot of that money was spent.

At the request of the brokers I interviewed for the exposés, I have changed the names of those involved and the firms they worked for. In the chapters on specific scams, however, all names of people and firms are real, taken from the public record. This book has an appendix, "A Context for Corruption," which gives the reader an overview of how the equities markets function—a context for the scams and manipulations that we'll explore in the exposés and the informational chapters.

So sit back, read on, and enter the intriguing world of the boiler rooms. Among other things, you'll learn that "the rip" is much more than just a kickback.

1

Life at Liberty and the Pursuit of Deviance

EXPOSÉ

Jason Genaro stared at the lead that his grunt cold caller had turned in to him on Tuesday afternoon. It was Friday morning. Genaro had been riffling through the stack of index cards the cold caller had submitted, each inscribed with a customer lead in bold black ink, when he came across this particular card. On it, centered at the top, were printed the names Lawrence and Cynthia Christiansen.

Scanning the card, Genaro learned that the Christiansens were conservative investors who owned a chain of Texas educational toy stores. But what really grabbed Genaro's attention was the couple's estimated net worth: $5 million, about half of it liquid. Not whales, but good, solid candidates. The problem was that such people were unlikely to bite at something as risky as Focal Point Technologies. Still, it was worth a try. Genaro picked up the receiver and dialed the Christiansen's number in San Antonio.

After a few rings, a woman with a clear, singsongy voice answered, introducing herself as Cynthia Christiansen.

"Mrs. Christiansen—hello," Genaro oozed. "This is Jason Genaro, senior broker at Liberty Capital Investments in New York City. How are you doing today, ma'am?"

"I'm fine," Mrs. Christiansen replied warily.

"Fantastic! Now, Cynthia, I know that my junior associate Tim Gardner contacted you last week, and he talked with you a little bit about your investment goals. I've just reviewed what you told him, and I think we can be of some assistance to you in meeting your objectives. Are you the financial decision maker in the family?"

"Well, not really," she admitted. "I'll get Larry. He's the one who spoke to your friend Mr. Gardner. Hold on, hun."

One of the things Genaro hated most about his job was being spoken to by prospective clients as though he was a college kid at his first job. Their patronizing tone angered him, but he'd learned to suppress his anger and prevent it from affecting his tone of voice. When it came time to pitch to the decision makers, he knew how to talk the talk.

"Larry Christiansen," boomed a gravely voice at the end of the line.

"Hey, Larry. This is Jason—Jason Genaro from Liberty Capital. Tim Gardner talked with you last week, and he suggested that I give you a ring and talk to you about some of your investment objectives. I know you're busy, so I'll be brief."

Larry Christiansen was very agreeable. Still, he insisted that despite the current strength of the markets—they were stronger, in fact, than he'd ever seen them—he didn't want to get mixed up in anything risky. He was a careful investor, and he was determined to maintain the long view, no matter how bullish things got. Genaro's adrenaline had started to pump. It was time to talk fast. He urged Christiansen to consider the need for diversification. It was crucial that he build diversity into his portfolio by picking up some of the more speculative offerings available to the savvy investor—like FCPT.

FCPT—Focal Point Technologies—was a California-based company that specialized in e-commerce. It had made its initial public offering (IPO) about a month earlier at about four dollars; it was currently trading at ten dollars. Genaro explained that the stock was moving quickly. Within two months, tops, he insisted, it would be pushing $20 per share. But Christiansen wasn't interested in FCPT. He would, however, give Genaro and Liberty a shot if they could come up with a proposal that felt right to him, but that proposal would have to be pretty solid if they expected him to entrust the firm with his money.

Genaro promised to fax Christiansen a proposal by Monday, adding that he would ensure that the investments it included matched Christiansen's investment goals. What Christiansen didn't know was that Jason Genaro never dealt in conservative investments. He was just talking the talk, speculating that if he could reel in Christiansen using some other kind of bait, he'd have bought himself some time to figure out how to get the wealthy Texan into FCPT.

FCPT was a house stock. About two months previously, Genaro had met with the board of Focal Point, Charlie "Chuck" Simmons, who was one of Liberty's owners, and Bradley Taylor, one of Liberty's primary strategic planners. They had discussed strategies that Liberty could employ to boost Focal Point's stock price. Taylor had been in the business for a long time, and he knew exactly how to run a profitable operation. He was strictly a behind-the-scenes player—he had to be, because several years earlier he'd been barred from the industry for life for manipulating a Canadian penny stock. For the same offense, Taylor was also hit with a fine of $10,000, but that meant nothing to him because he'd made almost a hundred grand from the deal. The lifetime ban didn't present him with much of a problem either. He just continued taking care of business without telling anyone—simple as that. The guys at Liberty knew that Taylor had the connections that could bring them the big deals, and they were only too happy to conceal his involvement.

The FCPT board members were up front about their intentions. They planned to sell off large chunks of their positions once the stock price had climbed. The Liberty people were very familiar with what the Focal Point people were asking them to do, and they were glad to oblige. Liberty would charge a cash fee, part of which would be used for broker incentives (kickbacks); the firm would also get an allotment of FCPT stock to supplement their own coffers.

The Liberty-FCPT meeting took place in September of 1999, when FCPT stock had already hit $10 a share. But the FCPT insiders saw the stocks of similar companies going through the roof on the back of the raging bull market, and they considered a $10 share price unacceptable. They were convinced that FCPT had the potential to hit $50, based on the market conditions alone. Although Focal Point was only doing minor business, companies with less impressive operational histories were selling like mad, and the FCPT guys were eager to recruit some experienced stock jockeys to help them capitalize on the situation.

A deal was hammered out, and it promised to be one of the most lucrative Liberty had ever been involved in. The stock traded on the OTC Bulletin Board (a regulated quotation service that provides investors with information on over-the-counter equity securities). It was a microcap—a type of low-priced stock issued by the smallest of companies—so there weren't many shares available. This meant that any increase in trading volume would bode well for the price of the stock, and given the prevailing market conditions, it would be easy enough for Liberty to hide FCPT trades by mixing them in with trades of legitimate companies like Microsoft and Motorola.

This was Genaro's plan for the Christiansens: first he'd get hold of their money, then he'd devise a way to use it for the maximum benefit of Liberty. As soon as he'd said goodbye to Larry Christiansen and hung up the phone, he fired up his computer and began surfing Morningstar.com—an Internet resource for stock quotes, analyses, ratings, and news—in search of some five-star mutual funds to recommend. He selected four that seemed to jive with the Christiansens' goals and printed out the stats. He knew how important it was that the proposal appear conservative. His conversation with Christiansen had clued him in to the fact that the Texan was a novice when it came to the markets and that he kept most of the couple's liquidity in a money market and in certificates of deposit at the local bank. The Christiansens didn't even have a broker; they dealt with a bank rep instead. For a man like Genaro, who for five years had been closing people far more sophisticated than the Christiansens, this scam would be a walk in the park.

It only took him an hour to cut and paste the Morningstar information into his own proposal, tailoring it to the Christiansen's profile. When the job was done, he buzzed his assistant, Laura, and asked her to fax the proposal to Texas. He also instructed her to call Larry Christiansen to confirm that he'd received it. Of course, Genaro could easily have made that call himself, but he'd learned that having a sales assistant, especially one with a sweet, feminine voice, call on his behalf gave the impression that he was much more professional and important than he actually was.

Laura was a hot young piece of ass he'd picked up at the biker-owned strip club just down the street from the brokerage house. He'd seen Laura dance on the club's stage and hired her to do a lap dance for him. Then he'd persuaded her to go out with him later in the week. Over dinner, he told her all about himself. He explained that he was the top-dog broker at Liberty, pulling in anywhere from $50,000 to $100,000 a month. However, he neglected to inform her that he came by most of that cash by working pump and dumps or by taking the spreads on excessively marked-up penny-stock underwritings—but, in any case, she wouldn't have understood what he was talking about. All that mattered to Laura was that Jason Genaro drove a tricked-out Porsche Boxter convertible and paid for everything. All that mattered to Genaro was that Laura was extremely pretty and sported enormous breast implants.

It wasn't long before Laura was begging Genaro for a job at the firm. She said that she needed to develop some practical business skills if she was ever going to get out of dancing. The idea appealed to Genaro—as the guy who had given her the opportunity to earn a respectable living, he would hold an important position in her life. And a grateful Laura would be more than willing to engage in workday sex acts that would help relieve his job stress as it built up. Genaro's office was located in a distant corner of the Liberty floor, and it had a heavy door that could be locked from the inside. The office would have been sound-proof if it weren't for the fact that the wall dividing it from the adjacent office was relatively thin. That office belonged to a new broker named Sean O'Brian who had just arrived from Boston bearing a good-sized client book.

As soon as Laura had faxed the Christiansen proposal, the scam was in motion. Genaro would wait a day before contacting the couple. This would give the Christiansens a chance to review the document; and, more importantly, it would allow Genaro himself time to imagine all the possible objections the Christiansens could raise and prepare his counter-arguments.

It was only lunchtime, but Genaro needed a drink. His buddy Bradley Taylor was an alcoholic, and Genaro knew he kept a good bottle of scotch in his desk. Leaving his office, he went out onto the floor where the firm's 100-plus frontline brokers buzzed away, phone receivers cradled between ear and shoulder—drones. To Genaro, this was the sound of money. As long as his retail force could keep selling, he'd keep making money. And to sell, they had to keep pounding those damn phones! This lesson had been drilled into Genaro when he was starting out in a similar shop in New Jersey. That's why, when he spotted a greasy-haired twenty-something sitting idly in his half-cubicle, he hit the roof.

Genaro had a short fuse at the best of times. He habitually behaved like an asshole whenever he could get away with it, and those beneath him in the brokerage hierarchy were fair game. Quickening his pace, he marched over to the unfortunate rookie, yelling towards Taylor's open door, "Brad! Get out here, we have a problem!"

The brokers within earshot, still gripping their phones, watched Genaro as he advanced on the kid. Taylor materialized, and as soon as he glimpsed Genaro hovering angrily over the young broker's desk, his lips twisted into a crooked smile. O'Brian referred to Taylor as "The Ghoul," partly because of this grim smile, which signaled his pleasure in the suffering of others, and partly because of his general physical appearance— Taylor was tall and gaunt and painfully thin, and he had a pallid complexion.

The horrified rookie stared up at Genaro. "What are you fucking doing?" Genaro yelled down at him. As his young victim stammered excuses—he was writing out a pitch, doing some quick stock research—Genaro just shook his head. He didn't want to hear it. His initial anger abated, and he began speaking to the rookie in a tone of controlled belligerence.

"Man, you have to pound the phones. You have to stay on the phones. It's a numbers game, bro. If you don't make the calls, you will never make it in this business."

Then, without taking his eyes off the rookie, Genaro called over to Taylor, "Get some tape, will ya?" Returning to his office, Taylor grabbed a roll of duct tape that was lying conveniently on the windowsill. He hurried back to the scene of the conflict and handed the tape to his colleague, anxious to witness the humiliation he knew was coming, ready for a good laugh.

"Pick up the phone," Genaro commanded the rookie. Hesitating for only a second, the trembling kid raised the receiver to his ear. Like a shot, Genaro grabbed his wrist and held out his arm. Ripping off a length of tape, he bound the rookie's hand to the phone, wrapping the tape around and around until only the kid's fingertips could be seen poking out from the big silver ball.

By this time, the other drones had abandoned all pretence of work. Stunned, they stood watching. Genaro, having completed his taping job, looked around at his audience and shouted at them to get back to work, but now his voice was full of suppressed laughter. Taylor and Genaro walked away from the cubicle bank, and, unable to contain themselves any longer, burst into hysterics.

They went into Taylor's office and shut the door. Recovering himself, Genaro asked for a drink, and Taylor happily withdrew a bottle of single malt from a cabinet behind his desk. As Genaro poured himself a neat scotch, Taylor went over to a golf bag leaning in the corner and extracted a shiny new club.

"Check out this new putter," Taylor said, passing it to Genaro. Taylor suggested that they try it out in the main room, so Genaro gulped down the rest of his drink, gripped the club, and followed Taylor through the door. Producing a golf ball from his pocket, Taylor set it on the floor. The two took turns whacking the ball across the thinly carpeted floor, until it finally bounced and flew over the low wall that separated the drones' cubicles from the rest of the room. It hit a young female employee working diligently at her computer. Laughing, the two top dogs ducked into Taylor's office again, avoiding identification.

Genaro and Taylor weren't the only characters at Liberty. There was also Tanya Stevens, a fairly successful broker with a solid clientele. While she brought in some good money, Stevens wasn't as greedy as the others. A woman of exceptional intelligence, she'd passed her licensing exam on the first try after only a few weeks of study. The 38-year-old former rock 'n roll party girl was exceedingly attractive to boot. She played the power game as well as the boys, and she had an appetite for the young rookies. Each month, she'd seduce two or three of these neo-phytes, most of whom were a good 15 to 20 years her junior.

Stevens's consorts were easily identifiable. They would fol-low her around the office like puppy dogs. Enthralled by this heavily perfumed succubus, they would neglect their careers. Most of the brokers who fell for Tanya Stevens ended up get-ting fired or failing the licensing exam, distracted and exhausted by the wild lifestyle that Stevens had led them into. And Stevens herself was wild. She described herself as a social drinker, and she was "social" almost every night of the week. While she enjoyed the limos and the top restaurants like the rest of her Liberty peers, her regular haunts were small bars and pool halls. She also liked the strip clubs, where she could indulge her lust for young women.

While Stevens tended to prefer guys, once in awhile she craved the soft touch of another woman, and when she did, she went hunting for it. She had discovered that her money made most strippers as affectionate towards their benefactor as men's money did—if not more so—so she added the local peeler joints to her list of hangouts.

On the afternoon that Genaro had bullied the rookie broker and he and his buddy Taylor had driven the balls down the fair-way of Liberty's main room, Stevens had a hankering for femi-nine attention. Seeking out Taylor and Genaro, she laughed halfheartedly at their antics and suggested that the three of them visit the local strip club later in the day. The guys knew about Stevens's tendencies, and they rather enjoyed watching her as she skillfully seduced the dancers. The two men proposed that they all meet at a nearby sports bar for a few drinks before head-ing off to the peeler joint. They set a time, and Stevens returned to her office. As she passed the miserable rookie with his hand taped to the phone, she flashed him a sympathetic smile.

By four o'clock, most of the top dogs had already split or were getting ready to leave, but Liberty was still crawling with supervisors, sales assistants, trainees, and the brokers who had been on the job only a year or two. These guys sometimes worked as late as 9:00 p.m. so that they could contact prospective clients in other time zones, like the West Coast and Hawaii. The more ambitious young brokers called their prospects continually. The realistic ones knew that it was all a numbers game, and they would work the phones hard, placing as many as 500 or 600 calls daily.

And once the bigwigs had ceased stalking the floor for the day, the drones could relax a little. Ties would come off and pranks would ensue. Occasionally, however, things would get out of hand. One evening, a former plaything of Tanya Stevens, affectionately nicknamed "Mouth Breather," started taking verbal jabs at another broker named Hopkins. Hopkins was a no-nonsense, nose-to-the-grindstone kind of guy. The only people he really respected were the senior brokers. To him, those who made money mattered; everyone else was insignificant.

Actually, Hopkins considered many of the brokers of his own rank or lower to be no better than hoodlums. He couldn't get over the firm's decree that even though clients never darkened Liberty's door, male employees must wear suits—simply because Liberty's owner, Chuck Simmons, believed that if you dressed for success, you were more likely to attain it. Hopkins would look around at his fellow drones in their ill-fitting discount-outlet suits (most owned only one), and his disgust would grow—hoods in cheap suits, that said it all. It just fueled his drive to join the ranks of the money makers and his determination not to take any shit from a drone. Hopkins never let the verbal abuse of his superiors distract him from his objectives, but if a broker of a stature equal to his own should attempt to interfere with him and break his concentration, then the former sewer worker would quickly become irate.

Now, Mouth Breather was not a small guy—he was over six feet tall, and he weighed about 230 pounds—but Hopkins stood several inches taller and was a solid 250 pounds. And Mouth Breather represented everything that Hopkins detested—he was a buffoon, an obnoxious loudmouth. So when Mouth Breather decided to lay into Hopkins, tempers flared.

To his credit, Hopkins did warn Mouth Breather to cut it out several times, but his nemesis paid no heed. He seemed compelled to keep telling Hopkins what a shitty stockbroker he was. So, after the third warning, Hopkins took action. Grabbing a phone in his huge paw, he yanked the cord from the jack and swung the device over the low divider that separated his cubicle from his tormentor's, bashing Mouth Breather in the head. The blow knocked him off his chair, and he crashed to the floor.

Supervising the junior brokers that evening was a guy named Ronnie Sands, a 32-year-old juvenile delinquent. As fate would have it, Sands was the one who had brought Hopkins to Liberty in the first place, as his caller. So, when his boy Hopkins clocked Mouth Breather with the phone, Sands just laughed hysterically and told Mouth Breather that he'd gotten what he deserved. Then he ordered everyone to "Get back on the fucking phones!"

Sands had been in the business for about three and a half years, and he was surprisingly successful at it. He didn't have the patience, contacts, or acumen to be a deal maker like Genaro, but he was one of the best salesmen in the game. When he was hot, he could easily open five accounts or more per day; in fact, he had to maintain this quota, because he lost a lot of clients after the second or third trade.

Fueled by cocaine—he had a $2,000-a-month habit—Sands was a wild man. He had no qualms about using while he was at work. He would sit at his desk in the far corner of the room, hidden by a partition, and slide out the writing-board extension. Conversing amicably with prospects and clients, he'd set up a few rails. His phone was equipped with an attachment that surrounded the mouthpiece, ensuring that the person he was speaking to could hear no ambient noise. Lifting the receiver away from his mouth for a moment, he could snort a line of coke and no one was the wiser.

On many occasions, upon opening an account, a completely wired Sands would leap onto his desk and face the floor, yelling, "I'm the best fucking closer in this fucking firm! Everyone else sucks!" Then he'd add, "Except for Hopkins—he's cool." Hopkins always smiled.

On the same day Genaro played the bully and Stevens got the urge to party, Sands, in one of his cocaine hazes, sat fidgeting at his desk. The phone rang. It startled him—most of his calls came in on his cell. He answered and heard Chuck Simmons say, "Hey, Ron." Returning the greeting, Sands held the receiver away from his ear for a second and gave his head a violent shake. He had to clear his thoughts. Simmons explained that one of the firm's biggest retail clients, a man named Ken Ackerman, was flying in from the Midwest that evening and had to be taken out on the town. Simmons himself had plans with his wife that he couldn't change, and he wanted Sands to take care of Ackerman.

Ackerman, he informed Sands, was a handful—he liked to party hard. Simmons knew full well that Sands was a user, but he didn't mind. He appreciated Sands's usefulness to the firm. The young salesman kept the boiler-room energy level up, and, despite his track record, he didn't actually lose much money for Liberty—most of the clients who fired Sands were simply transferred to (seemingly) more responsible Liberty brokers.

Sands said he was happy to oblige, and Simmons asked him to pick Ackerman up at his Lexington Avenue hotel at 8:00 p.m. This would allow Sands enough time to go home and grab a nap first. As he was leaving the office, he invited Hopkins to join the party that night. Hopkins accepted.

Driving home, Sands got a call on his cell from Genaro. That night, Genaro was going to hit a sports bar and then a strip club with his cohorts Taylor and Stevens, and he asked Sands to join them. They could let off some steam and watch Stevens in action. Sands's girlfriend was bisexual, and she occasionally brought girls home with her, so Sands was not particularly excited at the prospect of being an audience for Stevens. Still, it sounded good for a laugh—it would be funny to see Stevens throwing lines and cash at the strippers and to watch the other guys make fools of themselves like they'd never seen girls with girls before. He told Genaro that he'd be there and added that he'd be bringing Ackerman and Hopkins along with him. When Genaro heard Ackerman's name, he laughed. He'd met the man before, and he remembered what a sloppy drunk he was.

Hopkins showed up at Sands's apartment at around 7:00. He didn't usually snort coke with his mentor, but it was Friday night, and he was making headway with his career plan. He felt like celebrating. Sands racked him up a couple of lines and served him a cold beer. As 8:00 p.m. approached, they went down to the street and hailed a cab to take them to Lexington. The lobby of Ackerman's hotel was brightly lit, all plush and marble. Entering the bar, which they found just off the hotel entrance, they looked around for Ackerman. The place smelled of old wood and cigarette smoke, and it was practically empty. The only customers were a couple of middle-aged women and a solitary man who sat at the bar, clad in a black silk shirt, hunched over a whiskey and cola.

As Sands and Hopkins made their way over to him, the man rose and extended his hand. It was Ken Ackerman. An attorney turned CEO of his own PDA company, Ackerman liked to flaunt his success by wearing a Rolex watch and a thick gold neck chain. He was 47, but he gave the impression of being much younger—Hopkins suspected that plastic surgery had contributed to this effect. Greeting his hosts, Ackerman admitted that he'd arrived at the bar two hours earlier. He was already heavily buzzed, but he managed to remain quite coherent and pleasant. The two brokers, numbed by cocaine and beer, were humming along as well. They laid out the evening's agenda for Ackerman, chatted for a few minutes, and then headed off to the sports bar where they were to meet up with Genaro and his gang.

Sands's crew got there before Genaro's, and they settled into a black vinyl booth. Ackerman remarked that the cocktail waitress had a great ass and his two new buddies agreed, laughing. That loosened the vibe a little, but Sands was still unsure how to act with Ackerman—after all, he was one of Liberty's biggest clients, and Sands did not want to fuck up. It's true that Simmons had said he was a party guy, but Sands had no way of knowing whether that meant a few beers and some dirty jokes or major hell-raising. He'd have to feel his way through it.

It was soon obvious that Sands had worried needlessly. Ackerman confessed that although he was a married man, he liked to cut loose when he visited New York. Later that night, he'd like to invite, or hire, several women to a party in his hotel room—Sands and Hopkins were welcome to participate. Emboldened by this, Sands mentioned doing coke, and Ackerman responded enthusiastically. Things were looking up.

It was another half hour before Genaro, Taylor, and Stevens showed. Tricked out in a short black skirt and thigh-high spike-heeled boots, Tanya Stevens made a huge impression on the out-of-towner. He dropped the buddy-buddy attitude he'd adopted with his two chaperones and turned on the charm for Stevens's benefit. He motioned to her to slide into the booth next to him, and she graciously complied. But when Ackerman started trying out pick-up lines on her, she just laughed them off. She was still sober, and as far as she was concerned, the night was far too young for this. Besides, she had better options than the randy, drunken Ackerman.

While the others swapped stories and jokes, Genaro and Taylor had a hushed conversation about FCPT. They were pushing the stock hard, but they were uncomfortably aware that their clients would be expecting to take the profit on their FCPT shares very soon; if those clients triggered a selling trend, then the stock price would fall before Liberty could dump its own stockpile at a huge profit. And the last thing they wanted to do was stabilize the FCPT share price with their own inventory. Genaro mentioned to Taylor that if he could persuade the Christiansens to buy FCPT, that would be the push they needed to achieve a final run on the price.

Tiring of shop talk, the two co-conspirators returned to group conversation just as Hopkins was describing how, when he was a rookie, he and a couple of work mates had been jumped by a gang of skinheads one night in Wildwood, New Jersey. The junior brokers had beaten the hell out of the skinheads, cheered on by a crowd of onlookers. His story highlighted the vast differences between the "boutique broker," like Hopkins and his pals, and the wire house financial professional—the type of buttoned-down Ivy Leaguer most people imagine when they hear the word "stockbroker." The boutique brokerages, or "bucket shops," that spawned the likes of Hopkins tended to employ street-smart guys who had grown up relatively poor and had never attended university. They were neighborhood hustlers, and brawling with skinheads was not beyond the realm of their experience.

One asset these guys possessed as far as the firms that employed them were concerned was the ability to relate to clients of similarly modest backgrounds. And because these clients could relate to them, they could be persuaded to trust them. Trust was of paramount importance in the world of investing. Furthermore, wealthy clients liked these fast-talking wiseguys as well—through them, the staid investor felt connected to a more exciting lifestyle. So, all present found Hopkins's tale entirely credible—and very entertaining.

It was time to move on. But the group agreed that before they hit the strip club, they would drop in at a party that a friend of Taylor's was throwing at his apartment in a high-rise near Central Park. The man was the owner of another New York investment enterprise, but he had few retail clients. Instead, he'd built a niche for himself as a facilitator: he and his employees worked with market makers and short sellers to create and capitalize on stock-price movement.

Hopkins was new to this level of partying. This shindig was unlike anything he'd ever experienced. The apartment itself was exquisite—thick white carpeting, polished granite countertops, black glass tables. On three of these tables, illicit treats were laid out. One held a large sugar bowl and spoon; the bowl was filled with cocaine. Another held a plate of pills, which turned out to be Ecstasy. The third table bore a tray stacked with joints. Sands was in heaven.

It was about 10:30 when the Liberty gang arrived. All six of them were drunk. They helped themselves to the illicit treats— except for Genaro, whose drug of choice was alcohol. Stevens sweet-talked the initially reluctant Hopkins into ingesting some Ecstasy with her—he popped one pill; she popped two. Taylor went for the coke. He'd heard that Ecstasy ate holes in the brain, and he never touched the stuff. Sands, of course, went for it all. First, he snorted a couple of lines of coke. Then he threw back two E pills and fired up a joint. Ackerman kept right up with him—he was soon high on coke and stoned out of his mind.

Most of the male guests at the party were brokers or enter-tainment businessmen; most of the women were college students, strippers, or sales assistants. Tanya Stevens was the exception, as she generally was at these gatherings, because few women had penetrated this echelon of the chop-shop brokerage world. Sexual harassment, drug abuse, and obscene language were en-demic to this world, and most women were unwilling or unable to accept it.

By the time the Liberty crew left the party, those who had taken Ecstasy were just beginning to feel the effects. Everyone was drunker than hell. They managed to hail a cab, and Stevens ordered the driver to take them to the strip club. The establishment was renowned—it boasted some of the most beautiful girls in the city. Clubs like this rarely charge cover for women, so Stevens walked in for free. The men had to fork over $25 each—a reasonable rate for a "gentlemen's club."

Of them all, Ackerman was the most thoroughly annihilated. The doorman almost didn't let him in, but Genaro, a regular, dropped a lot of cash at the place, so the doorman finally relented and admitted Ackerman, warning Genaro to keep an eye on him. Genaro found a booth near the stage and shoved Ackerman into it, then Genaro and the rest of his cohorts made their way to the seats that ringed the stage.

The flashing lights and loud music were intensified by the drugs they had consumed. Soon, Genaro was completely entranced by the dancers slinking and rolling on the stage before him. The carnal display had mesmerized Taylor as well; he happily doled out cash to a curvaceous, topless blond who was shaking her well-toned backside in his face. For a while, Stevens watched with interest, but her main preoccupation was scouting out a sweet young thing of her own.

Sands and Hopkins sat next to each other, and Sands kept slipping his apprentice tip cash so he could keep the girls dancing in front of him, just like his top-dog companions. Everyone was having a great time, flying high and watching half-naked girls on parade. Then Sands remembered Ackerman, whom he'd left slumped in the booth behind them. He also recalled what Ackerman had said about finding some ladies who could be persuaded to come to a private party in his hotel room. But, turning around to invite the out-of-towner to join them stageside and select some stripper companions, Sands saw that the booth was empty.

Figuring that Ackerman had just gone to take a leak, he shifted his focus back to the stage. Ten minutes later, Ackerman still hadn't returned. Sands may have been blitzed, but he had the sense to worry. Simmons's important client was his responsibility, and there would be serious repercussions if he let him go staggering off into the city, drunk and alone. Excusing himself, he made several quick tours of the club, but he saw no sign of Ackerman. Finally, he asked the doorman if he'd seen him. The answer he got only heightened his drug-accentuated paranoia: about 20 minutes earlier, Ackerman had left the club alone and wandered away.

Fighting panic, Sands returned to his seat and filled the others in. Genaro and Taylor laughed and called him a dumbass for not keeping an eye on Ackerman. They reminded him, unnecessarily, that if anything untoward happened, Simmons would skin him alive. While Simmons was, for the most part, a calm individual, he was quite capable of becoming incensed. It was extremely unwise to provoke him.

Somewhat sobered by this turn of events, Sands headed out to look for Ackerman. Hopkins volunteered to go with him. Hailing a cab, they directed the driver to cruise systematically along the streets surrounding the club. As they set off, Sands was tormented by images of Ackerman being mugged and lying unconscious and bleeding in some alley.

They patrolled the streets for nearly an hour, running up a huge fare. All the while, Sands scanned the terrain through an open window of the cab. Finally, in the blue-lit doorway of a small bar, Sands spotted Ackerman, swaying back and forth and arguing drunkenly with a hefty doorman. Commanding the cab driver to pull over, Sands stumbled out onto the sidewalk.

Profoundly relieved, he yelled Ackerman's name. Ackerman turned around in surprise, startled out of his debate. When Sands suggested that they get into the cab and go back to the hotel, Ackerman readily complied.

Making its way through the streets of Manhattan, the cab passed throngs of night-lifers pursuing their own adventures and creating their own mayhem. The driver turned onto Lexington, and before long they were pulling up in front of Ackerman's hotel. Sands paid the exorbitant fare, and he, Hopkins, and Ackerman shuffled into the lobby. They rode the mirrored elevator to Ackerman's floor, and after some confusion, they located his room.

Sands broke out his last gram of coke, and, with Ackerman's permission, they began plundering the mini bar. The three sat around a table snorting lines and guzzling overpriced domestic beer. Finally, Ackerman pushed himself over his limit, and he passed out cold. At last, Sands and Hopkins were willing to call it a night, and they headed down to the lobby. Sands had to raid his wallet once more to give Hopkins $50 for the cab ride home. They said goodnight and went their separate ways.

Lying in bed the next morning nursing a hangover, Sands received a phone call. It was Ackerman. He'd had so much fun with Sands and his pals that he wanted to do it all over again that night. An astonished Sands, while seriously doubting that his body could tolerate it, agreed. They arranged to meet for dinner, and Sands prudently proposed inviting Simmons to join them— he was more than ready to shift the burden of responsibility for Ackerman onto his boss. He also hoped that the presence of Simmons would deter the depravity to some extent. Ackerman said that he'd call Simmons and extend the invitation himself.

Sands rarely saw Simmons socially, and when he did, either Genaro or Taylor was generally in attendance as well. That night, Sands brought along Hopkins, his usual sidekick, but he didn't bring along any cocaine, his usual stimulant. The call to his dealer could wait; stashed in his apartment was enough stuff to get himself up and functioning on Monday morning, and that was all he needed. Sands was still recovering from the previous night's outing, and he was hoping for a mellow evening.

And it was mellow. They dined at an upscale steakhouse near Ackerman's hotel, and during the meal Sands and Hopkins were uncharacteristically quiet, content to sit back and observe the interaction between Simmons and his client. Becoming a deal maker had never held much of an appeal for Sands. He loved the floor, and even when Simmons had offered him his own office, he had declined, preferring to remain in the trenches. He wanted to be where the action was.

He was intrigued at the way Ackerman laughed off the fact that Simmons had lost so much of the money he'd entrusted him with. It seemed that Ackerman didn't really care. He was sticking with Simmons simply because he and Simmons were like-minded fellows. The old saying, "People do business with the people they like, not with the people who are most competent," was especially true in this instance. Simmons knew how to relate to Ackerman. He was convinced that none of the "wire house pussies" would have the balls to work with Ackerman on his own terms and do the kind of trades Ackerman wanted to do.

In fact, Ackerman held a large position in FCPT. Liberty was using his account to boost the volume of the stock and maintain a steady price increase. Ackerman didn't know, and he didn't care to know. The money he placed with Simmons was gambling money, cash he could afford to lose. And Ackerman enjoyed playing the stock market much more than playing roulette in Atlantic City. There was nothing complicated about it—Ackerman just liked hanging out with the Liberty guys, vicariously experiencing the wiseguy lifestyle.

All of this made the unwitting Ackerman a prime target. His trust had been secured, he wasn't paying close attention, and Simmons could move in for the kill. Sands was beginning to understand the dynamic involved, and he knew that at dinner that night—despite his lack of interest in deal making—he was being presented with a golden opportunity to witness a whale being landed. A whale named Ackerman. Watch and learn.

When the steakhouse meal was over, Ackerman fought Simmons for the check, Simmons won, and the four men retired to the hotel bar for a few drinks. Ackerman asked Simmons to recommend an escort service—or prostitute dispatcher—and Simmons obliged with several referrals. It didn't strike Sands as odd that his boss was able to do this. In his mind, all inhabitants of the boiler-room subculture, from the top brass to the foot soldiers, had a taste for excess, and most were equipped to satisfy it in its many forms. And why not, as long as they had the cash to pay for it?

On Monday morning, Sands and Hopkins showed up for work ready to make some money. Sands wanted to compare notes with Genaro and Taylor about the events of Friday night, but Genaro didn't seem to be around. He dialed Taylor's extension, and when Taylor picked up, they fell into conversation. Taylor said that after Sands and Hopkins had left to hunt for Ackerman, he and Genaro had each bought a couple of lap dances, but they kept lapsing into shop talk—particularly on the subject of FCPT. Stevens, flying high on party drugs and booze, had scouted effectively, netting a petite blond named Stacy, who had long, curling locks. The young stripper was excited about being pursued by the attractive, middle-aged professional. When Stevens started simulating oral sex on the girl in front of the crowd, a bouncer told her she'd have to take it into the VIP area. Stevens needed no convincing. After Stacy had completed her set, Stevens beckoned to her. The two whispered and giggled, much to the amusement of Taylor and Genaro, and they eventually retired to the curtained-off VIP section.

They remained behind the curtain for almost a half an hour, and when they emerged, Stevens returned to sit with her colleagues, who were still stationed at the edge of the stage, drunk and high and talking business. Stacy's last set wouldn't finish for another half an hour, a flushed Stevens reported. As soon as Stacy was done, she was going to take the hot young thing back to her place—did they want to wait around too, or go their own way? Genaro and Taylor opted to stick around.

The four cabbed it back to Stevens's swanky Lower Manhattan residence. Her ninth-floor apartment was modern and sparsely furnished with expensive, stylish pieces. The decorating scheme included several expensive-looking crystal figures sculpted by a local artist. Genaro and Taylor sank into the couch, and Stevens crossed an expanse of blond-wood floor to a wet bar.

Stacy followed and stood behind her, caressing Stevens's back as she poured four vodkas. Anticipating a good show, Genaro and Taylor sat sipping their drinks, but the vibe mellowed out for a while. Stacy leaned against Stevens, occasionally stroking the older woman's leg. For some reason, this restrained display of intimacy turned the men on more than anything else they'd seen that night. Finally, Stevens went to get something from the kitchen, and Stacy followed her. After they'd been gone for several minutes, Genaro urged Taylor to go and find out what was keeping them. Taylor discovered the two ladies kissing passionately.

Unfortunately for the enthralled Sands, Taylor's story ended there, because it was at this point that Stevens declared it was time for her colleagues to leave. Stacy giggled.

Sands was outraged. He couldn't believe that the tale had been cut off at such a critical point! Taylor proposed that they corner Stevens and pry the dirty details out of her. Sands enthusiastically agreed, but the opportunity to interrogate Stevens never presented itself. Around noon, Stevens rushed out of her office, on her way to meet Stacy at Liberty's main entrance. She was gone for the remainder of the day. Genaro was still nowhere to be found.

Genaro didn't return to the office until the following day. On Saturday, he'd dropped by Liberty to pick up some paperwork. While there, he'd found the Christiansen's faxed reply to his proposal. They just loved what he had thrown together—this only confirmed their naiveté—and they wanted to meet him in person. Genaro had called them immediately. Larry Christiansen was pleased to hear back from him so quickly, and he was very impressed that the broker was in the office on the weekend. They talked for nearly half an hour, and Christiansen informed Genaro that he was prepared to spread $1.3 million over several of the recommended mutual funds, but he would really like to meet the broker face-to-face before making such an investment. They set up an appointment for Monday afternoon at the

Christiansen's San Antonio home. The moment he hung up, Genaro dialed his travel agent, booked a flight, and reserved a hotel room for Sunday night.

The meeting with the Christiansens took place according to plan. Genaro stressed yet again the conservative nature of his proposal and assured the couple of his dedication to the task of meeting their investment objectives. Of course, Genaro had brought the necessary account forms with him. He helped his clients fill out the forms and complete the wire-transfer documents. Everything was set to go. On Tuesday morning, Genaro strode across the sales floor and into his office, hollering triumphantly. The $1.3 million was on its way. Now all he needed to do was wait an appropriate amount of time before using that cash to move some more FCPT.

By the end of the week, the Christiansens' money was in their Liberty account. Genaro promptly carved it up, buying into the mutual funds he had selected for his new clients. Then he called Larry Christiansen to tell him that everything had been taken care of and Laura would be sending out the trade confirmations that day. The waiting game began.

About three weeks later, Genaro again contacted Christiansen. He told him that the mutual funds were performing well, but he predicted that some potentially more profitable and equally stable investments would be hitting the market within the next few weeks. He requested discretionary authority over the account so that he could take advantage of any golden opportunities that presented themselves in the timeliest possible fashion. "Do whatever you think is best," Christiansen replied. This verbal consent was just what Genaro had been angling for. He was actually surprised that he'd obtained it so quickly and easily.

On the day the next monthly account statements were mailed out, Genaro liquidated the Christiansens' mutual funds and bought heavily into FCPT. He spent every last cent of their money loading up on the stock. Things were going very well. In fact, the pump was working so well for Liberty that everyone involved stayed in a bit longer than they had originally planned. So, when the Bloomberg stock-reporting service issued a press release questioning FCPT's legitimacy, the conspirators were caught off-guard.

Only a week after Genaro had taken action with the Christiansen account, Liberty sold off its entire proprietary account. The FCPT insiders who had initially approached the crew at Liberty to pump the stock sold off their vast holdings as well. The price plunged from nearly $60 per share to less than $10. Genaro had bought the Christiansens' shares at close to the peak price, and the couple suffered staggering losses—nearly all of their liquid assets had been ravished by the dump. An equally staggering amount of money made its way into the accounts of the crooks.

In the weeks following the FCPT dump, life at Liberty went on as usual. Genaro and Taylor began looking around for their next deal. Then reality came crashing in on them.

At first it seemed like any other Friday afternoon. The floor was buzzing, rookie stockbrokers and trainees shouted their pitches—a well-rehearsed rap passed down from seasoned broker to green recruit—and slammed down their phones. Then Genaro, sitting at his desk, heard a strange, harmonized murmuring, mixed with random expletives, emanating from the floor. Suddenly, Taylor was at his door: "Dude! Flip on MSNBC!"

The puzzled Genaro picked up the remote to his office TV set and flicked the channel from ESPN to MSNBC. The network was broadcasting live from the floor of the New York Stock Exchange. The NYSE is a permanent bedlam, but today the general commotion was clearly more intense than usual. The steady stream of ticker symbols running along the bottom of the TV screen was punctuated with red downward arrows. Everything was dropping, and not just incrementally.

The bubble had burst. The infamous crash of 2000 was under way. Genaro and Liberty's other top dogs had seen dips in the market, but nothing like this. As the markets plunged, the Liberty accounts, most of them margined to the max, were driven into negative equity, causing Liberty's clearing firm to freeze Liberty's ability to trade. As the days passed, Liberty's floor drones split into factions; camaraderie disintegrated. Many brokers were simply there one day and gone the next. Their desks were ransacked for any leads or account forms left behind in haste. The phones rang off the hook, but most of the brokers were reluctant to talk to their clients. Genaro was one of them.

One Monday morning, he arrived at work to find Larry Christiansen waiting for him. Laura had tried valiantly to keep Christiansen off the floor, but he'd stormed past her and located Genaro's office himself. Catching sight of Genaro, he marched over to him and started chewing his broker out for avoiding his calls. The big bearded Texan was angry, and he didn't even know yet that he'd been totally screwed over.

Calmly, quietly, Genaro coaxed Christiansen into his office. There, he explained that things had been exceedingly hectic, what with the crash and all, and he apologized for being too busy to return his calls. Christiansen wasn't buying it. It had been almost two months since he'd received an account statement. Now he was demanding to see documentation of the state of his account. Fighting panic, Genaro realized that he couldn't talk his way out of this one. He buzzed Laura, asking her to print out the relevant statement and bring it in.

For a long time, Larry Christiansen perused the document without uttering a sound. Then he looked up and fixed Genaro with a furious glare. When he spoke, his voice was low and controlled. It chilled Genaro to the bone. He declared that he would be staying on in New York until it was clear to him what the hell had happened. He was true to his word. Each morning, he would be waiting for Genaro when he showed up for work. Genaro was profoundly unnerved by this—and by everything else that had gone down—but there was little he could do about it.

Simmons called a meeting of his top guys: Genaro, Taylor, and O'Brian. He informed them that Liberty was under assault: an audit had been ordered; the SEC had subpoenaed documents; the firm had been hit by a number of FCPT-related civil suits. Simmons ordered the brokers to use their private lines and cell phones only, and he told them that he was letting the support staff go.

Within a week of that meeting, Liberty had vanished without a trace, and its top dogs had gone into hiding.

2

Prime-Time Pump and Dump

Bill Stanley is the sole owner of a new construction company. Arriving at the office at 6:00 a.m., the 42-year-old entrepreneur spreads the sports page across his desk and settles in to read it while sipping coffee from the cup of his metal thermos. The phone rings. The following conversation takes place.

"Bill Stanley, please," says a confident voice.

"Speaking."

"Mr. Stanley, this is Joe Stockton of First United Equities Corporation. Listen, Bill—one of our junior brokers spoke with you a few months ago, and you said it would be okay for us to get back to you when we had a business idea that was worth your while. Well, something just came across my desk this morning that I think you'll be interested in. Do you have a pen, Bill?"

"N-no," Stanley stutters. He's a bit confused. He doesn't remember the call from First United, but he receives so many calls of this type that he can't be sure. Sometimes he blows the caller off; other times, if he's in a good mood, he gives him a chance to make his pitch. The name First United Equities doesn't ring a bell, but who knows? Fumbling around on his desk for a moment, he finds a pen and paper.

"Okay, got one."

"Great! Bill, the company we're buying today is called National Medical. It trades on the OTC market. Have you heard of it?"

"No. Can't say that I have."

"You will. So will everyone else, and very soon. Bill, this is a ground-floor opportunity—almost as good as getting in on an IPO. Imagine getting in on Microsoft at the very beginning of its growth, or Pfizer right before it announced Viagra. Wouldn't that have been fantastic?"

"Well, yeah . . ."

"No kidding. And this is exactly that kind of opportunity. National Medical has just been acquired by a major holding company with a lot of cash to put into it. Besides that, National is the owner of several biotech patents, and it's poised to make some incredible breakthroughs in genetics within the next year. Now is the time to buy this company, before the public gets wind of it and drives the price up."

"Listen Joe, I'm not really buying anything right now. I'm reinvesting most of my money in my own company. But thanks for the call."

"Bill, I completely understand where you're coming from. You work hard, and you want to grow your business, but this isn't some piece of shit stock I'm bringing you. This is the best company I've seen in a long time. I'm buying it for all my clients, even my family and friends. If you never buy a stock from me again, then so be it; but you don't want to miss the boat on this one, Bill. Now, I understand that you're hesitant, but let's just start with a small position—say $50,000?"

"You know what, Joe? I already have a broker."

"I'm sure you do. Every sophisticated investor has three or four brokers. Give the guy some competition! Use my performance with National as a standard for judging any other broker you deal with. You've never done business with First United before, correct?'

"Correct."

"And if we were to work together, you would naturally judge my effectiveness based on our first transaction, correct?"

"Sure. Of course."

"Then let's make this happen, Bill! Listen, I've been sitting on your information for almost four months now, just waiting for the right opportunity. Well, National Medical is *it*, Bill. I wouldn't bring it to you if it wasn't a money maker, would I? I mean, if you make money, then I make money. Plus, I make my living on building a client base. I count on repeat business, and if I don't bring my clients the best deals, then I don't make a good living. Does that make sense, Bill?"

"Yes."

"All right, then! I'll put you down for 10,000 shares. It's just under five bucks a share, so it will only come out to about 50 grand."

"Wait, Joe. I didn't say I was going to buy anything yet."

"Oh, for Christ's sake, Bill! If a squirrel ran up the leg of your pants would he starve? Where the fuck are your balls! I thought you were a businessman."

"Look Joe—I *am* a businessman, and I don't have to listen to your bullshit!"

"Yeah, I know. I'm sorry. Listen, please don't mistake my enthusiasm for pushiness. It's just that I really believe in this stock, and I don't know when I'll be able to bring you another opportunity this good. Tell you what—First United gets three or four IPOs a year. Do you like IPOs, Bill?"

This piques Bill's interest. He's read newspaper reports about people making loads of money on IPOs. He doesn't quite understand how they work, but he knows that getting in on an IPO is a difficult thing to do.

"Well, sure," says Bill. "Who doesn't?"

"Okay, I'll tell ya what. I usually reserve IPO allocations for my best clients, because that's where my allegiance is, but I also know that this first transaction we're doing is on good faith, so the next IPO I get, I'll make sure you get first crack at it. Does that sound good to you?"

"Okay. That sounds good, but I only want to buy 2,000 shares."

"Are you kidding me, Bill? Did we just go through all of this for a measly 2,000 shares? Bill, I don't deal in those low numbers. Are you telling me you've just wasted my time here?"

"Listen, I just don't want to take on such a big commitment without having a chance to check it out first."

"I'm sorry, Bill, but I've spent a long time working my way up in this business, and I didn't get to where I am today by bringing shitty stocks to my clients. I haven't worked at the 2,000-share level for years, and I'm just not willing to take a step backwards. My minimum transaction with this deal is 10,000 shares. But I promise you that this stock will go up, and in a big way. I'm telling you there is absolutely no risk here—that's how confident I am. Between you and me, I have information that I can't divulge. I mean, because of my position, I'm privy to things that the public is unaware of, and let me tell you, Bill, this is a sure thing. But I guess I misread you, Bill—it seems like you can't really afford this opportunity."

"If I make this trade, you can get me in on the IPOs?"

"Absolutely. IPOs are for our preferred clients. If you buy 10,000 shares, you'll definitely qualify as such."

There is a long, tense silence. Bill is filled with nervous excitement, and his mind is reeling. Joe is dead quiet. Bill breaks the silence.

"Okay—let's do it."

*   *   *

Many investors have received a call like this one. Except for Joe's verbal guarantees, there is nothing illegal about it. The style of telemarketing he employs is called "high-pressure sales" by the SEC, and it's the norm for boiler-room brokers.

Although the conversation between Bill and Joe is fictitious, the sales tactics it illustrates were utilized in a classic pump-and-dump scheme undertaken by three firms: First United Equities Corporation (of Manhattan, Garden City, and Woodbridge, New Jersey), the apparent lead brokerage in the scam; Lexington Capital (of Hauppauge, Long Island); and AGS Financial Group (of Manhattan and Chicago). The scam was devised and headed up by four ruthless manipulators: Gregg Adams, Jonathan Winston, Jason Cohen, and Michael Reiter. They were eventually charged by the U.S. Attorney's Office with fraudulently manipulating the stocks of five companies: Ashton Technology Group; EquiMed; IRT Industries; Mama Tish's Italian Specialties; and National Medical Financial Corporation.

Adams, Winston, Cohen, and Reiter gained control of EquiMed, IRT, and Mama Tish's through prearranged trades and through various financial incentives from the control people of those companies; the IPOs of Ashton and National Medical were underwritten by First United. Once the group had control of the shares of the companies, they set up shop and started pumping the prices.

From the aforementioned brokerages, the manipulator group solicited customers in a retail sales push that involved unregistered brokers and cold callers. The brokers and callers were encouraged to misrepresent the potential and the operating performance of the companies. Like Joe Stockton, they made two promises to their clients: they would give them access to deals; and they would guarantee that the stocks they were selling would show a profit in the future. It was illegal for them to make either promise.

The brokerages held the stocks of the five companies in their own inventories, and they sold them directly to their clients. Between May of 1996 and November of 1997, the share price of each offering rose steadily: for example, Ashton hit $15.25, EquiMed shot to $16.50, IRT climbed to $7.25, and National Medical went to $13.50. But these highs were entirely attributable to the manipulators' sales push and the actions they took to support the prices of the stocks.

The strategies they employed included verbally abusing clients who wanted to sell their shares of the pumped stock; if the client placed a sell order anyway, the manipulators would simply neglect to process it. They would also threaten clients with physical violence if they engaged in any activity—such as short selling—that would undermine their plan. In addition to this, brokers involved in the scam would make unauthorized trades within their clients' accounts. In one case, a broker even purchased stock for a deceased client.

The pump was phenomenally successful. Once the stock prices stabilized, the manipulators marshaled their forces and launched the dump phase of the operation. Along with certain company insiders who were privy to the scam, they started to unload their positions in the five companies en masse. The effect of the dump was reflected in the stock prices of the companies as of March 2001, the month the indictment of the manipulator group was unsealed: Ashton was listed at $1.94, EquiMed at $.03, IRT at $.04, and National Medical at $.00.

The indictment identifies the duration of the operation as February 1994 through March 1998. It charges 20 people, including brokers from the three boiler rooms, with implementing the scam. According to the investigating authorities, investors were scammed out of approximately $50 million over the course of the operation. They further alleged that Adams and Reiter were associated with the Mob—specifically the Gambino crime family. Said Barry W. Mawn, assistant director-in-charge of the New York FBI investigation: "In addition to describing the pump-and-dump tactics and boiler-room schemes allegedly engaged in by the defendants as they committed the traditional white-collar crimes of securities fraud, wire fraud, and mail fraud, this indictment also identifies two associates of organized crime." Mawn went on to explain that because actions undertaken by law-enforcement agencies had eroded organized crime's control over its traditional sources of income, the Mob had branched out. Securities fraud was one of the areas that mobsters had begun to penetrate.

Several forces coordinated their efforts to bust the operation: the New York State Attorney General's Office, the U.S. Attorney's Office, the FBI, the SEC (which, on March 8, 2001, filed an enforcement action against 18 individuals for using boiler-room tactics to defraud investors), and local law enforcement. Commented New York State Attorney General Eliot Spitzer, "This is really a case of life imitating art—it's a combination of *The Sopranos* and *Boiler Room*. Unfortunately, it's not the movies or TV, it's real life and we have real victims—thousands of them—who combined have lost $50 million. This was a classic 'pump and dump' case where corrupt brokers gained control of worthless stocks, illegally inflated their value, and then sold their shares at enormous profits, leaving their victims holding the bag."

A less complex illustration of the pump and dump can be found in the alleged actions of Ilan Arbel (an Israeli citizen residing in New York) and David Melillo (of Saint Petersburg, Florida). The two manipulated the stock of an Arbel-owned company called Hollywood Productions (later renamed Shopnet. com). The SEC's complaint alleges that Arbel, a known operator of publicly traded shell companies, provided Melillo, the principal of a brokerage called Euro Atlantic, with large amounts of Hollywood's stock at deep discounts. Melillo set up a retail frontline of brokers at Euro Atlantic—which the SEC described as "in essence a boiler room"—to peddle the stock. The first step was to sell the IPO.

Even though the investing public was still shell-shocked from the market crash of 2000, the buzz word "IPO" struck a

chord of hope in the hearts of many. Besides charging both
Arbel and Melillo with using high-pressure sales tactics and
conducting unauthorized trades, the SEC charged Melillo with
placing conditions on investor participation in the Hollywood
IPO. A number of large, established investment banking firms
are currently under investigation for the same offense—coerc-
ing a participant in an IPO to purchase shares of the same security after the company has gone public in what is termed the
"aftermarket."

The SEC alleged that Arbel and Melillo controlled the
demand for, and the price of, Hollywood through "fraudulent
and deceptive sales practices." These practices included instruct-
ing brokers to refrain from executing sell orders for Hollywood—
dumping the stock during the pump phase of the operation
would have sabotaged the scheme. The commission further
alleged that Euro Atlantic's brokers were paid kickbacks—rips—
on sales of Hollywood stock. Since these "sales commissions"
were not disclosed to the clients, they, too were in violation of
federal securities law. On August 21, 2001, the U.S. Attorney's
Office officially charged Arbel and Melillo with conspiracy to
commit securities fraud in an operation that bilked investors of
nearly $8 million.

The Hollywood Productions case is a relatively straightforward one. The litigation releases of the regulatory agencies
involved and the case files of the investigating authorities contain numerous examples of similar schemes, many involving the
same illegal tactics. The primary perpetrator in one particularly
egregious case was an IRS attorney turned tax lawyer named
Max Tanner. His scam defrauded more than 300 investors of
$3.7 million.

Tanner (whose son Daniel has been charged with paying homeless people in San Diego to fight for a video he coproduced and sold called *Bumfights: Cause for Concern*) masterminded a pump-and-dump scheme that utilized boiler rooms in New York City and Boston and a brokerage in New Jersey. The scheme took shape in 1996, when Tanner gained control of a publicly traded shell company.

After obtaining the shell, he incorporated a company he called Maide Aide. The Maide Aide operation was simply this: one woman cleaning the offices of Tanner's co-conspirator, stock promoter Donald Evans. Tanner then merged a Florida-based outfit called CFE Trucking with Maide Aide and established a ticker for the new company: MDAN. Through the merger, Tanner and Evans gained control of MDAN's publicly traded stock. Tanner set up a brokerage account in Canada and used it to funnel the securities through the boiler rooms to the investing public.

A boiler room's function is to be a site for pitching and selling stock to the public. The better the salespeople on the boiler-room phones, the more stock gets sold and the higher its price goes. Tanner's brokers, many of whom were unlicensed, used all the usual hard-sell tactics, successfully pushing MDAN to hundreds of investors. Tanner paid his frontline brokers kickbacks, and, as the primary perpetrator, he scored nearly $10 million from the pump-and-dump scheme. To avoid paying taxes on his illicit profits, Tanner established a company in the tax haven of the Cayman Islands, naming it Delta Financial Resources.

But, unfortunately for Tanner and Evans, certain activity patterns triggered by the scheme had alerted the industry regulators. The SEC and the NASD noted the rapid spikes in the price and volume of the stock and called for an investigation. Eventually, Max Tanner was indicted on 37 counts of securities fraud, mail and wire fraud, money laundering, and tax evasion. On November 8, 2002, he was sentenced to an eight-year prison term. He was also ordered by the SEC to pay restitution of $2,145,167, plus $350,000 in civil penalties, and $616,000 in interest. Evans was also convicted in the scam, but the presiding judge granted him another trial. The SEC barred both men from ever serving as an officer or a director of a publicly traded company.

*   *   *

The cases I have just described share a number of fundamental similarities. For one, the manipulators who devised and worked the scams used boiler-room sales tactics to pump the stocks. The typical pump-and-dump fraudster creates the illusion of urgency to push potential clients into risky situations. He pressures his victims to decide, and decide *now*—no time to think. Exploiting an investor's fear of blowing the chance to become rich by hesitating to act, he fires off the classic boiler-room line, "I've been in the business a long time, and in my experience I've seen more people lose more money from indecision than from a bad decision." But seasoned investors and honest brokers know that to make a sound investment decision, you first have to weigh all the factors and examine all the angles—and this takes time.

The first crucial step that the average pump-and-dumper—like the ones who appear in this chapter—must take is to gain control of publicly traded companies whose stocks have a low daily market volume. Control is the most important aspect in any securities scam. Without it, the fraudster's ability to manipulate securities is severely limited. So is his potential for turning a profit. There are two basic ways for an individual or group to gain control of a company. The first is by creating or finding a suitable company and taking it public in an IPO—an initial public offering. The second is to gain a controlling position in a company through an acquisition—a merger or a takeover.

Within the field of investment banking, there are other means of bestowing large blocks of stock upon individuals or groups, but the IPO is by far the most lucrative for the insiders of a corporation. When a privately owned company needs a cash injection, one of the best recourses its principals have is to take it public. This means placing the company on one of several stock markets, making it available for trade. The cash injection comes from the underwriter, also called an "investment banker" or a "venture capitalist." The shares released to the market are called the "float"; the company that is going public is called the "issuer." The underwriter initially purchases the float from the issuer, temporarily supporting the stock price when the stock hits the market. The public offering price is the price that investors must pay for the stock; the underwriter pays a lower price, called the "underwriter's spread," and this is how the underwriter earns a cut of the deal. The underwriter's spread can sometimes be as high as 25 percent of the offering price.

In most cases, the underwriter isn't a single firm or invest-ment banker—a group of firms, called a "syndicate," will share the risk of the new offering. The syndicate elects a manager to act on behalf of the group; the manager is usually the firm that the company wishing to go public first approaches.

After registering the security, establishing the underwriting terms, and forming the syndicate, the syndicate manager appoints a selling group, whose primary responsibility it is to distribute—or sell—the IPO. The selling group may consist of the syndicate and as many as several hundred dealers.

One of the manager's foremost responsibilities is to stabilize the stock price of the now-public company once it hits the open market. This process is called "pegging," and it involves the manager bidding up the price of the stock. Pegging is strictly regulated by the SEC, and it can only be conducted during the offering period, which usually lasts 30 days. The underwriter buys enough shares on the open market to prevent the stock price from dropping below the public-offering price, but after 30 days, this practice is no longer legal and the underwriter must desist. Sometimes, this results in a radical price drop, depending on how investors have taken to the issue and how well it has been distributed by the selling group.

Although the IPO is the most widely recognized and approved activity in the control game, acquisitions are equally important to those who want to control a corporation's destiny. The most common form of acquisition among securities fraudsters is the merger.

In its most basic sense, the term "merger" means a combining of two or more companies in which only one of the companies survives or bears the name of the new entity. In other words, when the dust settles after a merger, only one participant remains standing. There are two standard types of merger: the "pooling-of-interests" merger and the "purchase" merger.

In the first type, the itemized assets and liabilities of the companies involved are simply mixed together—hence the term "pooling." It's a desirable approach to merging companies, because the transaction is tax-free, but in order to be legal, the transaction must conform to certain rules. Each participating company must prove that it has been autonomous for two years before the merger and that it has never owned more than 1 percent of the common stock of any of the other companies. The merger must be accomplished as a single transaction, or it must be the end result of a plan implemented within one year. The surviving company—also called the "acquiring company"—is obligated to issue its common stock in return for 90 percent or more of the common stock of the other companies. Finally, for a minimum of two years, the acquiring company is prohibited from doing the following: reacquiring the common stock issued in the merger; entering into any deals for the benefit of its former stockholders; and disposing of large amounts of the assets of the other companies participating in the merger.

If all of the merging companies are able and willing to fulfill these conditions, then they may undertake a pooling-of-interests merger. If they can't, then they must resort to a purchase merger. In this scenario, the acquiring company has to purchase all assets of the target companies—at their true market value—and add them to its own. Should the acquiring company pay more than the fair market value for these assets, then it must list that premium on its books as "goodwill"; goodwill may be written off incrementally over a period of 15 years.

Such premiums are paid in purchase mergers for the intangible assets of the acquired companies—that is, assets that don't have quantitative or liquidating value. These might include: a brand name or recognizable product name; a history of customer satisfaction and service; or a highly motivated and effective employee base. Intangibles like these give the acquiring company a higher earning potential.

Some companies that want to go public have difficulty meeting the listing requirements of the various stock exchanges. Some are reluctant to hand over equity control to a venture capitalist or investment banking firm. Companies such as these have the option of going public without subjecting themselves to the underwriting process: they may arrange to be acquired through what is called a "reverse merger."

The cornerstone of the reverse merger is the "shell company"—a company whose balance sheets show zero assets and zero liabilities. Essentially, it's a hollow shell. Only the corporate structure remains. Like an abandoned shell lying on a beach, it may be found and inhabited by a new entity. A company desiring to be traded—a new entity—can take over a corporate shell, acquiring the shell's structure and market listing, thereby executing a reverse merger.

A private company looking to go public via reverse merger begins by hunting for a suitable shell. There are pitfalls in this process, like the "dirty shell"—a shell company within which creditors and/or shareholders lurk. The new company, with its fresh cash supply, moves in, and the creditors and shareholders launch claims against it. It is therefore important for the company seeking to go public to locate a "clean shell"—often referred to as a "blank check." The clean shell has no claims against it; it is simply a corporate structure that fulfills the listing requirements of the various stock exchanges. Many clean shells are actually set up for the sole purpose of being sold to shell-seekers.

As we've seen, fraudsters use shell companies—those they've moved into, or those they've set up themselves—to gain a foothold in the market and launch their scams. Once they've amassed a majority of the common stock within the shell, they can start manipulating the stock price using frontline brokers, press releases, and the Internet.

A reverse merger is transacted when a minimum of 51 percent of the stock of the private company (the one that wants to get listed) is handed over to the shell company (the one that is already listed) in return for 51 percent to 90 percent of the shell's common stock. Basically, the shares of the shell are converted, becoming shares of the new entity. The shell is now inhabited, and the new occupants may file the appropriate paperwork to change the name—and the ticker symbol—of the shell. Voila! A new public company is born.

This is how a company with no operational history or assets or revenue can begin trading. What follows is the story of how one such company attempted to play the shell game.

*   *   *

As 1998 dawned, Original PSA was a privately held startup airline with only one airplane. Its principals wanted to raise money in order to expand and grow their business. Since the company had no operations to speak of, it would be incapable of attracting venture capitalists, so its principals had to find a different form of financing.

Original PSA looked to a group of "financial professionals" called the First New Haven Corporation, led by one Edward J. Durante. After meeting with the First New Haven group, the Original PSA people decided to implement the technique of the reverse merger. Their plan was to gain access to a market, sell shares in PSA, and raise money for growth. The first thing Durante's group had to do was to search for a shell company into which they could back Original PSA. They also purchased leads—lists of proven investors—to use when it came time to pump the price of whatever shell company Original PSA wound up in.

To effect the reverse merger, Durante enlisted two consultants: Mark Gould and Jackson Morris. Gould consulted with First New Haven on a structure for the reverse-merger transaction, and Morris drafted many of the documents essential to the deal. (According to an SEC litigation release dated April 3, 2001, Gould was paid 100,000 shares of the post-merger entity, PSA Incorporated, and Morris was paid 50,000 shares of the "new" company.)

First New Haven located an attractive shell company in Nevada, called American Telecommunications Standards International, which was trading on the OTC Bulletin Board under the ticker symbol ATSI. In March 1998, Durante's group met with the CEO of ATSI, Thomas K. Williams, to execute ATSI's acquisition of Original PSA. Their plan was to house the startup airline in ATSI, change the name to PSA Incorporated, and begin promoting the stock. Part of this transaction involved Williams transferring roughly 2.1 million shares of unregistered stock to First New Haven. As arranged, First New Haven undertook to distribute the shares on the open market. Williams would receive a cut of the proceeds—that is, a kickback. The reverse merger was complete. Now they had to drive the price of the new stock as high as possible.

It is important to note here that securities law prohibits the sale of unregistered stocks—if a stock is registered, then a filing for it exists. The law further prohibits the offer of a securities sale unless a registration has been filed. No registration was ever filed for the transfer of the new entity's stock to First New Haven, nor was there any registration filed for the stock used to compensate Gould and Morris.

Shortly after the pump was started, PSA's stock price rose quickly, hitting the five-dollar mark by the end of March. In April, First New Haven began dumping its position. The price plummeted to less than one dollar. Durante alone pocketed over $325,000 for less than four months' work. But the fraudsters' greed did not subside. In May, they hired an online stock touter, Timothy Pinchin (who in 1996 had been barred from the Canadian securities industry for insider trading), to pump the price of PSA yet again.

They paid Pinchin, who ran a website called Insiderwire.com, 125,000 shares for his efforts. On his site, Pinchin made false claims to lure investors. One such claim was that only 457,000 shares of PSA were available to trade. In truth, First New Haven alone controlled nearly five million tradable PSA shares. Then there was Pinchin's assertion that the stock, which had dropped to about a dollar, was really worth between six and eight dollars. However, shortly after receiving his allotment, Pinchin began selling off PSA for less than a buck. Go figure. Gould and Morris also sold off their positions. All involved were in direct violation of federal securities laws. The SEC and federal law-enforcement agencies are investigating them and filing actions against them.

*   *   *

In each of the cases described in this chapter, fraudsters accomplished a pump and dump by commandeering large amounts—controlling positions—of a given company's securities. The pump and dump is the most straightforward form of securities fraud, and elements of it may be found in almost every other type of scam in the industry.

3

The Control Freak and the Jumped Gun

EXPOSÉ

It was a warm spring day in April of 2000. A stocky man in his mid-thirties and a buxom blond wearing a skin-tight business suit with a very short skirt ducked through the doorway of a small San Diego pub. The dimly lit establishment, called Bob's Dive Bar, hardly seemed the appropriate setting for an important business meeting. But the man—Daniel Powers, stockbroker turned dealer—wouldn't consider going anywhere else. Bob's was his favorite local meeting place.

For one thing, he was on friendly terms with Bob, and Bob allowed him to bring along his underage sales assistant/girlfriend—Kimberly, the buxom blond, 14 years his junior. Powers liked to have Kimberly with him at his business meetings, because he'd discovered that prospective clients were easier to deal with when she was around. Besides, it was better than having his coked-out cohort Nick Lorenzo there with him.

That April day, Powers was meeting with representatives of a company called ProLine, and it was a particularly important occasion. If he closed a deal with ProLine, he could be taking home close to a million dollars.

Powers's appearance reflected his dive-bar sensibilities. His usual business attire consisted of T-shirt, surfer shorts, and flip-flops. This approach to dressing he referred to as "stealth." He was undercover—no one would suspect that he was pulling in more than $100,000 per month. And Powers applied this stealth approach to his business dealings as well.

A couple of years earlier, frustrated with the workaday grind, Powers had decided to quit working as a plumber and pursue a more lucrative career. His wife, Darla, the daughter of a prominent local businessman, was eager to help him realize his ambitions. She contacted her brother, J.P. Gunderson, a partner in a boutique brokerage called Del Mar Securities, and J.P. agreed to meet with Powers to discuss the possibility of bringing him into Del Mar. This meeting would alter the course of both men's lives.

It was 1998, and the stock market was booming. Everyone, from doctors to housewives, was "in the market." Many had three or more brokers whom they never even saw in person— they placed their trades over the phone. It was a no-brainer market. Stock picking was a cinch—it didn't take a financial whiz. Almost everything was on the rise; you could pick a few at random, and the majority would be winners. It was a perfect time for a plumber with big dreams to get his feet wet.

Powers met with Gunderson, an excitable and persuasive man of questionable business ethics, and Gunderson painted a rosy picture of the investing world for him. The plumber with the hungry heart was hooked. This was just what he'd been looking for.

Powers had come from a relatively modest background. He yearned for the freedom that money could buy. He lusted after all the usual things: the season football tickets, the cases of beer, the fancy restaurants, the fast cars and beautiful, attentive women. He envisioned himself traveling to rock concerts in the back of a limousine. Mundane greed. And Powers was not overly concerned about what he had to do to get these things. His singular lack of ethics gave him something important in common with Gunderson, and Gunderson was pleased to bring his brother-in-law aboard.

The first thing Powers needed to do was amass a client base, so Gunderson started him out as a trainee at Del Mar. Like any other rookie, he'd be paid $1,500 per month, and he'd pound the phones from 6:00 a.m. to 6:00 p.m., studying for the licensing exam in any spare moments he had. It was a grueling schedule, and the immediate rewards were small, but Powers was encouraged by the fact that he had a distinct advantage over the other trainees. Gunderson had taken him under his wing and was showing him how to set up the deals that made the real money—the deals that entailed transferring heavily discounted stock into the brokerage's inventory and collecting the difference on the spread.

Now all of this was perfectly legal, but it was also heavily regulated by the NASD. Specific guidelines dictated the amount a dealer could mark up a stock for sale to the public (no more than 5 percent), and all such stocks had to be registered and cleared for sale—that is, unrestricted. These regulations limited Gunderson and many of his kind in terms of how much money they could make and how fast they could make it. In other words, the rules of the game were unacceptable.

Getting around the markup wasn't too difficult. Clients who were busy making money would not jeopardize the situation by asking questions. And without client complaints to act upon, the NASD seemed content to turn a blind eye. The problem of stock registration was circumvented by using offshore accounts, typically in the Cayman Islands or Costa Rica, where banking and securities laws are invitingly lax. The dealer—in this case Gunderson—only had to deposit restricted stock in an offshore account and liquidate it from there; the proceeds would remain in the account, sheltered from taxation.

Once assimilated into the brokerage's inventory, the stock at the center of a given Del Mar scam could be held, sold, or bought back, depending on how much activity Gunderson wanted it to display. This strategy is called "painting the tape," and it is highly illegal. Once the mechanism for manipulating the stock price was in place, the next step would be to pump the price as high as possible. This is where the brokers—the sales team—would come in.

Del Mar would call on all of its brokers to assist in the scam. The rip, or kickback, would be established, and the sales team would be set loose on the phones. When the price reached an acceptable level, the dealer and the insiders involved in the scam would cash out their respective inventories, causing the stock price to sink like a stone and leaving the clients holding the bag.

By watching Gunderson at work, Powers learned the intricacies of orchestrating a pump and dump. He also learned how easy it was to scam clients who were making money in other investments. Another vital lesson Gunderson taught him was that in the over-the-counter (OTC) market, the listing requirements for companies were so relaxed that just about any outfit could go public. In fact, a company barely needed to exist—it just had to have filled out the necessary paperwork.

Powers started to hatch a plot. They could create their own company and take it to market. Why should they go through a middleman (another company) and be forced to share the profits when they could simply create and incorporate their own publicly traded company and own the entire inventory? He presented the idea to Gunderson, and his mentor was happy to provide him with all the guidance he needed to pull it off.

A hip sports clothing company seemed like a good way to go. Clothing was generally an easy startup, and they could do some minor local business and get a little local press coverage to lend the enterprise an air of legitimacy. So that's what Powers settled on. He started the paperwork required to bring the thing to market and asked a few friends if they wanted to be part of his new company. Those who agreed signed on as directors of the corporation. Powers himself was a director as well. Things moved along quickly, and soon Power Surfwear was ready to go public. It was all surprisingly simple.

In 1998, the mere chance of getting a piece of an IPO could trigger a buying frenzy among the investing public. It was the perfect time to launch Power Surfwear. It debuted on the market under the ticker symbol SURF, and the scam was up and running. Powers and Gunderson controlled everything—Power Surfwear and Del Mar, the brokerage that was selling the IPO— but that fact was never disclosed to investors.

The IPO was a resounding success. The IPO price of a dollar rose to $2.50 in just a couple of days. Powers kept up appearances by doing a small amount of real business, but the sales figures and earnings he reported to the investing public were completely false. The price continued to climb. By the end of the second month, Gunderson and Powers were able to sell off thousands of shares, pocketing hundreds of thousands of dollars each.

Powers had been with Del Mar for eight months and his monthly income had risen to upwards of $50,000 when everyone involved in the brokerage became aware that their activities had attracted the attention of the local press and the NASD. Someone had discovered that one of Gunderson's partners was operating without a license, and Gunderson himself was soon facing an investigation related to filings he'd made on a transfer several months before the SURF IPO. In fact, the NASD had been following Del Mar's activities for some time. Powers's dream come true was rapidly becoming a nightmare.

He met with Gunderson one afternoon at a local sandwich shop to discuss their predicament. They agreed that their best course of action was to shut down the entire operation. They'd close up shop and lay low. By midnight, they had broken down the entire brokerage; the documents and computers had been moved to secure locations and the brokers and support staff had been let go.

Gunderson went underground, traveling to Costa Rica, but Powers remained in San Diego. He'd only had a small taste of the business, and he wanted more. There is a saying in the industry: "Bulls make money. Bears make money. But pigs get slaughtered." Powers would have been wise to have heeded this adage, but instead he took the money he'd acquired at Del Mar and purchased his own brokerage house, Pacific Capital.

This brings us to that April meeting between Powers and the representatives of the Florida-based ProLine. Powers had already laid out his plan for Jonathan Casey, the CEO of ProLine, and while Casey was reluctant to go along with it, he was finding it hard to say no because ProLine's stock price had dropped from $40 a share to just under $10. Much of Casey's own stock was already cleared for sale, but he was greedy: he wanted to see it move a bit before he sold out his position. He was ready to talk business Powers-style.

The two parties had actually worked out many of the details of the deal in advance of the Bob's Dive Bar meeting. What remained for them to do was sign the transfer forms and reach a decision about the discount that Powers would receive—the deeper the discount, the more cash would go into his pocket. Powers knew that he had to give his brokers at least their typical rip, which was a dollar per share sold; he also aimed to pocket a minimum of two bucks per share himself; and, ideally, he wanted a small margin to maneuver with. Taking all of this into account, he made Casey an offer to buy at $5.

As he expected, Casey didn't go for the first offer, but after a few rounds at Bob's, Kimberly's cleavage began to work its magic. Casey finally agreed to unload 500,000 ProLine shares for $6 apiece. Powers would be able to move the price and maybe even have enough to dump later at the full market price. In any event, he foresaw a million-dollar potential profit for several months of work. The three toasted the agreement and settled into small talk.

When it was time to leave, Powers paid the bill and left a hefty tip. Despite his greed, he wasn't a miser. On the contrary: he spent his money freely. Once, when he was courting Kimberly, he had left a cab with the meter running for over an hour while he took her on a shopping spree. The fare had been $300. Needless to say, his youthful sales assistant had found this display, and others like it, very seductive.

Leaving Bob's, the trio made a plan to meet up later that night for some celebrating. Powers and Kimberly walked to the parking lot where his convertible Mercedes was parked. "Hey, Kim," Powers said, "I think I want a Ferrari. Would you start checking out models and colors?" He enjoyed assigning her these little tasks. Although he had no intention of buying a Ferrari, he liked to reinforce Kimberly's perception of herself as essential to the business, and somehow even mindless missions like this one made her feel important. On one occasion, he'd asked her to be the creative consultant for a Web page design he was doing for an online sports company, even though Kimberly had no Web experience whatsoever. He went so far as to tell her he would give her 50,000 shares when the company went public. She always believed him and happily fulfilled his requests.

The two climbed into the Mercedes, and Powers drove the few short blocks to Pacific Capital. He was grossly out of shape, and he detested physical exertion of any kind—except, of course, for his romps with Kimberly. Pacific was located in an outdoor mall next to a burrito shop, identified only by some discreet lettering on its glass front door. Most passersby never even noticed it. That was exactly the way Powers wanted it.

"We got the ProLine deal!" he announced as he walked in. The handful of brokers occupying Pacific's front office gave a rowdy cheer. These guys were extraordinary salesmen who worked long hours and didn't ask questions. But Powers didn't like them much—they were too loud and abrasive.

Nick Lorenzo appeared, wiping some crusty white residue from his right nostril. "Right on!" he said. "What's the rip going to be?" When Powers replied, "The usual," Lorenzo was pleased. That meant a buck a share, and he knew that since he was the most senior broker he would have access to as many shares as he wanted. He turned his attention back to the project he'd been working on before Powers had returned—convincing the new sales assistant, Tara, to get naked for cash.

Powers laughed at his friend's antics, remembering the time he had taken Kimberly to a peeler joint and convinced her to accept a lap dance from a salacious brunette stripper. He'd liked that—it was about control. While he loved having lots of money to buy things, he was learning that he enjoyed something else that money could secure for him even more. Cold hard cash bought control. Powers had come to believe that without control, you were just some bitch penny stockbroker or caller who wouldn't last a year in the business.

Gunderson had shown him that the key to the big money—and the real control—was deal making. Getting paid in both cash and (unregistered) shares was the way to go. The cash allowed him to pay his brokers the rip and put some quick money in his own pocket. But the shares, when he eventually unloaded them, represented the real jackpot, especially if his sales guys did their part and got the price moving.

Powers himself would always help nudge the price in the beginning. Using a proprietary account to buy and sell the stock and create the illusion of legitimate volume worked nicely in this regard; most of the time he only had to do this for a week or so before the stock price popped. Most of these scams lasted just a month or two, tops. Powers had launched Pacific Capital with $50,000, and within a year he'd made over $2 million. Not bad for a plumber without a university education.

In fact, his success had convinced him that people who went to college were idiots. Kimberly had started attending classes at a community college, but he'd soon put an end to that. Anyway, he hated the idea of her hanging around with college guys who would hassle her for her phone number. So he promised her that if she dropped out of college, he would make her his partner in an online shopping business that he was going to take public. He told her he would give her 100,000 shares of the company, and that it could go as high as five bucks per share after the IPO. This empty promise was more than enough to persuade the gullible 19 year old to pack up the books. Problem solved.

It never ceased to amaze Powers how women responded to money. He had always been a bit overweight, and until he had made it in the investing business he hadn't been much of a ladies' man. Years earlier, he'd hung out with a heavy-metal rocker crowd, and he could never convince the kind of girls he dated now to give him the time of day. The difference was simple: then he was poor; now he was loaded. He still went to rock concerts, but now he rolled up to the venue in a limo. He always had a babe on his arm, and he always sat in the front row.

He was married, to Darla, and they had two small daughters, but for the first time in his life, Powers was desirable to women, and he was taking full advantage of it. Darla hated his lifestyle, but she felt powerless to change it. Anyway, she herself had grown accustomed to the kind of life his money could buy for her, and she wasn't going to compromise her position.

Kimberly was the second personal assistant Powers had slept with. The first was Angela, a tall, thin blond. She had been crazy about him, and she had been his best girl. He'd taken her to concerts, and he'd treated her to dinner every night. Like Kimberly, Angela would do all sorts of crazy things in the bedroom to impress Powers and hold his interest, but Kimberly had walked into the office one day looking for a job, and that was it for Angela.

Kimberly was much younger and far more impressionable than Angela. She was also in awe of Powers, and this gave her boss's ego a big boost. Powers, in Kimberly's eyes, was a business genius. It hadn't occurred to her that he was a scam artist, and when the newspapers eventually started publishing reports on his illegal activities, Powers was able to convince her that it was all a pack of lies—a certain reporter had it in for him. Kimberly was just 19, and she was having the time of her life; she wanted to believe what her sugar daddy was telling her, so she did, ignoring all indications that he was involved in shady dealings.

Early in their relationship, Powers—ever the control freak—had begun dangling the money carrot in front of Kimberly's nose. She had started out as the receptionist for the entire firm, but by her first company Christmas party, Powers had decided to bag her. He'd said as much to Lorenzo. So he established the pattern of making Kimberly feel important as a means of controlling her. He told her he was going to San Francisco to resolve some issues with Pacific's clearing firm, and he'd need her "help" while he was there. When he overheard her calling her friends and saying, "Guess where I'm going!" Powers knew she was a pushover.

Powers waited to make his move, though. He wanted to be sure that he'd succeed. When he took Kimberly to Las Vegas to party with some wealthy clients who owned a racing-car company, he knew he had her hook, line, and sinker. The helicopter ride to the desert and the nice hotel room had bowled her over—but still Powers bided his time. He'd begun to enjoy the game. Back home in San Diego, he decided the time was right to make his move. By then, she was far too impressed with his lavish lifestyle and his business acumen to resist. A moth to a flame. When Powers asked her to be his girlfriend exclusively, she readily agreed.

Everything did not go smoothly after that, however. Powers soon realized that Kimberly didn't yet know her place; he'd have to show her. One night, Powers had to entertain an important out-of-town client. He was well aware that this client loved strip clubs and the girls who worked in them, but he failed to explain the approach he intended to take to Kimberly, who would be accompanying them on their night out. Powers wanted to use Kimberly to impress his lascivious client, but Kimberly thought the outing was a purely social thing—just a few drinks and some fun. So, when they got to the club Powers had chosen for the occasion, she wandered off to chat with some friends she'd spotted in another part of the club. After awhile she got bored and came to tell Powers and his client that she was leaving. Powers was furious. Hadn't she grasped that she was his trophy girl and it was her duty to make him the center of her attention?

In a rage, he followed her out to her car, berating her for her stupidity. Why had she failed to be his bimbo? Why had she screwed everything up? Understanding, at last, what was going on, the humiliated Kimberly burst into tears, but Powers was unmoved.

The next day, Kimberly called Powers to apologize. Of course, he forgave her—the sex was too good not to—and things returned to normal. Powers was confident that his lovely young Kimberly wouldn't leave him as long as he kept providing her with an exciting lifestyle. She had grown up fairly poor, and she'd always had to work hard for everything she got. Now that she was dating Powers, she wanted for nothing, and she seemed prepared to pay the price: total obedience. If a friend of hers did not meet with Powers's approval, that friend was history. If Powers wanted her to stay at home on a particular evening— even if he himself was otherwise engaged—she canceled her plans. If she slipped up and got a little assertive, Powers's confidence remained unshaken; if he even hinted that he might dump her, she'd back right down. He had ultimate control. It was almost too easy.

Through all of this, Powers still slept with Darla. He loved his kids and didn't want to upset their family life. Besides, his daughters were young, and by the time they were old enough to understand what he was up to, he'd probably have finished sowing his wild oats. And another factor bearing on his decision to leave well enough alone was that if he left Darla, she'd claim half his ill-gotten gains. Kimberly had started bugging him about divorcing his wife, but he easily put her off by telling her that he had tried several times to file for divorce, but Darla was refusing to countersign. Fortunately, Kimberly was unaware that it only took one party to initiate divorce proceedings.

After announcing his ProLine success to his Pacific Capital employees, Powers made his way through the brokerage's front office to a locked door at the far end of the room, the docile Kimberly at his heels. Fumbling with his keys, he found the appropriate one and entered his office. His sanctuary. No one was allowed inside without his permission. Even his phone line was separate from Pacific's network. Powers required absolute privacy to think and to plan his deals. He'd seen so many of his counterparts destroyed by their own loose tongues and blustering egos, and it had made him secretive. Kimberly was the only exception—he allowed her to hang around his private office— but she didn't have a clue what was going on anyway, and it was great to have her on hand as a midday stress reliever.

Things were working out fantastically. Besides ProLine, Powers had three other deals on the table. Plus, he was in the process of forming a corporation that he could take public. All the companies he worked with were OTC Bulletin Board or Pink Sheets offerings. Those services were the only ones he could use to make the kind of money he wanted, because they listed the small companies. These companies didn't have to file annual reports with the SEC, allowing fraudsters like Powers to fabricate glowing operational histories for them. Powers had done it with SURF.

Powers made money in a variety of ways. Sometimes he acted as a promoter, sometimes he set up investment banking deals for small companies that needed quick cash, and sometimes he underwrote startups that he thought his brokers could sell to the public. If he could use it to channel cash into Pacific's accounts, then he'd do it.

He liked dealing with other companies because the cash and stock payoffs were good, but he liked starting out with his own corporation even better because he could issue himself a lot more shares than anyone else would. He was excited about the corporation he was now planning. He would reverse merge it with a shell company he had recently purchased and get the money train rolling right away. He had made Kimberly and his cousin Thomas officers of the corporation. A board stacked with people who knew nothing about business or the markets meant no hidden-agenda bullshit—Powers was ensuring himself a free hand. Despite the old adage, there was no honor among the thieves who populated the investing world. Powers knew that back-stabbing was common, and he didn't trust anyone with intelligence and experience.

His lawyer, Mark McGovern, was the sole exception. McGovern had worked in the area of corporate law for over 10 years, and he knew all the loopholes. Powers could level with him about his schemes and ideas because his confidences were protected by lawyer-client privilege. This made it possible for him to sit down with his lawyer and hammer out ways to make money while openly discussing the legal ramifications. He only regretted that McGovern hadn't been around during the SURF operation—especially now that some old problems related to it had started to resurface.

Apparently, some SURF investors had complained to the NASD. Unbeknownst to Powers, the NASD and the SEC had been tracking his activities since Del Mar had vanished. The SURF IPO had put Powers on the regulators' radar. They were watching everyone who had been associated with Del Mar very closely—especially those who owned their own brokerages. And Powers's position was weakened by the fact that he'd begun to believe in his own hype: he was convinced that he was a shrewd deal maker, not just some con artist. He was proud of the way he'd manipulated the prices and percentages—the fact that it was illegal was merely a technicality and not worth thinking about too hard. Neither did he bother to think about the tragic human cost of his actions. Greed had made him monstrously self-absorbed. Shortly after Powers and his crew had dumped SURF, one Del Mar client had killed himself, and in his suicide note he'd blamed his drastic stock market losses.

Powers had heard that a former Del Mar broker had been arrested on unrelated charges, and he wondered what it meant for him. But he couldn't let things like this shake him—he had business to conduct. He was scheduled to fly to Boca Raton in early May to discuss a deal with a pharmaceutical company that needed a quick cash injection. He also had to pick up some stock certificates in Las Vegas as compensation for a stock promotion he was currently working. There was a lot for him to think about, and he had to force the investigation out of his mind.

Nick Lorenzo was another concern. He was an extreme cokehead and a hyperactive jerk on the phones, but outside of the office Powers found him fun to hang out with. Recently, however, Lorenzo had been getting into blow more heavily, and this worried Powers—not because he feared for Lorenzo's health, but because he was worried that the unlicensed Lorenzo would get busted and work some kind of plea bargain. He was a liability. Still, Lorenzo was the firm's biggest producer, routinely bringing home $100,000 a month. He could sell the shit out of anything, and Powers needed him to drive up prices in his investment banking deals.

Nothing thrilled Powers more than seeing the price of his inventoried stock climb daily to its peak and then hearing Lorenzo, jacked up on adrenaline and coke, yelling, "Do it! Hit it! Now! Now! Now! Hit it!" Those words heralded the dump of the stock in his accounts and the resolution of weeks of work on the part of his sales team. It was profoundly satisfying.

Kimberly's hot mouth on the back of his neck snapped Powers out of his reverie. It seemed like she was always horny.

But before he could get anything interesting started, the phone rang. It was his old friend and former boss, J.P. Gunderson. He was back in town. Powers hadn't heard from him since he'd gone underground in the wake of Del Mar's collapse.

Gunderson had holed up in Costa Rica, one of the tax havens they'd exploited during their Del Mar days. They had rerouted their restricted stocks there and hidden their illicit earnings from the prying eyes of the IRS there. Costa Rican banks operated under a blanket of secrecy rivaling that of the Swiss banks—those who kept money in Costa Rican accounts could remain nameless, referred to simply as "anonymous societies." Many of the nation's banks were owned by German corporations, but this didn't seem to affect Costa Rica's viability as a tax haven. Powers himself had over $1,000,000 stashed in various Costa Rican accounts, and Gunderson had substantially more.

Gunderson hadn't been idle in exile, and he wanted to show Powers what he'd been up to. He told him to boot up his computer and go to this Web address: worldsecuritiestrading corp.com. It was the site for a business he'd established. It had occurred to Gunderson that there was money to be made providing the global investment community with a means of participating in stock offerings available all over the world. The system was still in development, but he would be bringing it to market soon. He wanted to raise enough funds to get the thing off the ground.

It sounded interesting to Powers, but he already had plenty to worry about. And now there was something new. What if Gunderson's reemergence in California caused the regulatory agencies to intensify their investigation? Powers informed his former co-conspirator that the heat was most definitely still on from Del Mar and that he probably shouldn't have returned. Powers explained that he, himself, couldn't leave, or he would have. He had a wife and two kids to think about. They would never consent to run with him, and he wasn't about to leave his daughters. Powers also admitted to Gunderson that McGovern had told him he was the less culpable party in the Del Mar fiasco—on paper, at least—because McGovern could make it look like he was set up to take the fall. Gunderson replied that despite the risks involved in showing his face in San Diego again, he couldn't stand to stay in hiding forever, and he had his own attorney going over the case.

The legal advice Gunderson had received so far was that even if he was arrested, he'd likely get off with a fine. Both Gunderson and Powers were unconcerned about being hit with a fine—it was the prospect of jail time that rattled them. The two chatted awhile longer, and then Powers said he had to go. He asked Gunderson to stay in touch. He didn't say so, but he wanted to keep an eye on his brother-in-law—J.P. wasn't above betraying a relative and colleague to keep himself out of jail, if it ever came down to that. Powers invited Gunderson to come to the house for dinner a couple of nights later, and he hung up the phone.

The weeks passed, and everything seemed normal. The ProLine stock came in as scheduled, and the cash appeared in Powers's account. The Pacific sales team got to work on the pump, and in two weeks they drove the price from just below one dollar to over five—in an unstable market! His guys really were the best. Powers used a portion of his inventory to stabilize the price as his brokers drove it up. Finally, when the price hit seven dollars a share, they pulled the trigger. It was as easy as that. Powers banked a huge profit and decided that after his May business trip to Florida (with Kimberly) he'd take some time off and enjoy the summer.

Kimberly, always on the lookout for exciting new ways to spend Powers's money, discovered that Ozzfest—a heavy-metal extravaganza—was touring North Carolina at about the time they had to go to Florida. She easily convinced Powers to spring for the tickets. They'd catch the fest and continue on to the Sunshine State. Kimberly booked the flight to North Carolina, and through Powers's ticket broker, she purchased the Ozzfest tickets. Powers never accepted anything less than fifth-row seats, and to get seats like that you needed a ticket broker. The broker quoted Kimberly a price of $400 a pop, and she went ahead and bought the tickets without consulting Powers—she knew that such prices were routine for him.

After partying at Ozzfest, the two headed off to Boca Raton, where Powers would hook up with the folks at CelluTech, the cash-poor pharmaceutical company. Powers met with the CEO and the CFO in CelluTech's small corporate offices to discuss what kind of discount they could offer him on the stock. The stock was only worth about $.23, and Powers wanted a discount of at least 30 percent. He promised the CelluTech reps that Pacific could pump the price high enough for them to make money when they sold off their own shares, and after some haggling they agreed to a 25 percent discount. The company needed around $200,000, so Powers purchased several hundred thousand shares at the negotiated discount. The stock was transferred to a Pacific account three days later.

But market conditions were still declining, and summer was a traditionally slow season for the industry. Powers would have to pump the CelluTech price fast if he was going to make any money on the deal. And, given the initial low price of the stock, he was only able to offer his brokers a reduced kickback. It was barely worth their while.

Powers's thoughts again returned to that summer vacation he'd planned after the success of the ProLine scam. He decided that now was the time—he'd let the guys handle the CelluTech pump, and he and Kimberly would go and ride motorcycles and ATVs in the desert. Palm Springs was only a few hours away, and it had some nice resorts that weren't too far from the dunes where he liked to ride. He was a big fan of off-road vehicles, and he owned a couple of them. All the money he spent on recreation, on wining and dining Kimberly, on flying around the country, on concert tickets and limos, came straight out of the pockets of thousands of investors. Many of these people were far from wealthy, but they'd bought the dream of wealth that his brokers pushed. To Powers, it was all just business—he was making money, not taking money.

As the hot summer days came and went, it became obvious that the CelluTech effort was not working. People were wary of the markets. Speculative offerings—like those listed on the bulletin boards—made them especially nervous. If the situation didn't turn around, Powers would have to sell off his shares in December and take a loss. Still, it was no big deal. Losses looked good on paper and diverted suspicion from his offshore shelter.

In July, one of Pacific's top traders, Peter Woo, had expressed an interest in buying the firm from Powers. He'd made a lowball offer, and Powers had turned him down. But now Powers was beginning to harbor serious doubts that the market would recover anytime soon; furthermore, the scrutiny of the regulatory bodies was starting to wear on him. Suddenly, Woo's offer looked interesting. Powers decided to sell the shop and get out while the getting was good.

Also, Kimberly was getting uppity as the summer progressed. She was hanging around other guys. She assured Powers that these men were just friends and that her loyalty was to him, but he no longer felt that he was the center of her world. It made him very uneasy. It also made him angry. When Kimberly wasn't with him, he was consumed with anxiety—who was she with, and what was she doing? Kimberly was slipping out of his control, and control was everything.

Towards the end of August, everything began to catch up with him. One Tuesday night, McGovern called him on his cell to tell him that Gunderson had just been picked up by the feds. It was likely part of a sweep, his lawyer said, and that would mean they'd be coming for Powers as well. Two days later, McGovern called again. By this time, Powers had gone into hiding, laying low at a friend's house an hour outside of town—he wasn't planning to bolt, he just needed time to get his head together. McGovern wanted to meet with him in person to discuss the options. Powers was being sought on charges of securities fraud, conspiracy to commit securities fraud, money laundering, and tax evasion—all extremely serious allegations.

Over the course of their professional relationship, Powers and McGovern had worked out explanations for many of Powers's questionable actions, but the wire trail and Powers's undertakings while at Del Mar weren't so easy to cover up. McGovern advised his client to turn himself in to the local authorities and go through the arraignment process. He'd be released on bail, and then it would be at least two years before the case went to trial. During that time, McGovern and Powers could prepare an adequate defense or explore other ways of handling the situation. Powers accepted his lawyer's advice and returned to San Diego to turn himself in.

The sweep netted four Del Mar brokers, all of whom had been involved in the SURF IPO. The story made the local evening news, much to the embarrassment of Kimberly, but this, and a few articles published in the local paper, was all the attention the sweep received. As McGovern had predicted, Powers was released on a $150,000 bond. He attempted to resume his normal life, but he was troubled by the fact that Kimberly's passion for him had cooled. She was distant, and he was suspicious.

Powers knew the password to Kimberly's e-mail account, and he decided to use it. He needed to know who was getting the attention he felt was rightfully his. It turned out to be a very informative exercise. He learned that she'd been sleeping with one of her men "friends" for, he guessed, at least two months (it had actually been over six months—the entire time she'd been seeing Powers). Powers felt panicked by this information. She'd been playing him—she'd been the one in control, and he hadn't even realized it. He couldn't stand the thought of losing her. She was his, and her affections were his territory.

So he picked up a 12-pack of beer, went to her house, and let himself in with the key she'd given him a long time ago. He waited and he drank. By the time Kimberly showed up, at about 6 p.m., Powers was drunk. She greeted him with a smile and a hug, but he pulled away and handed her the printout of the telltale e-mail. She yelled at him for invading her privacy, but he deflected this argument, telling her that the only reason he'd snooped was that she'd made him suspicious—and, furthermore, his suspicions had been justified. Kimberly countered this with some surprising information.

Over the past several months, she had received calls from Darla and angry messages from Darla's friends. They'd called her a home wrecker and a whore. They'd also told her that her lover had been sleeping with his wife, even though he'd sworn to her that he wasn't. Powers was caught off guard by this news. Suddenly, he'd lost his advantage. Suddenly, it was apparent that Kimberly had had a legitimate reason for pulling away.

Powers scrambled for a new approach to the situation. He did not want to lose Kimberly—at least not yet—and in his desperation he came up with the idea that they could consider it a compromise. They were now even, he insisted. They'd both lied and cheated, but now that everything was out in the open they could start again on a foundation of honesty. He professed his undying adoration and promised her a future of travel and adventure—all expenses paid. Kimberly was as reluctant to lose her meal ticket as he was to lose his plaything, so she agreed to give it another try.

He could regain absolute control over her, Powers was sure of it, and he was delighted at the prospect. He told her that he'd only slept with his wife out of guilt. When he asked Kimberly what had motivated her to sleep with someone else, she burst into tears. She maintained that the man had gotten her drunk and taken advantage of her; then he'd manipulated her into a sexual relationship that she hadn't wanted. She tearfully promised to have nothing more to do with him. Her tactics worked beautifully on Powers, who still had no idea that she'd been sleeping with the guy the entire time she'd been dating her boss.

Powers was under the impression that the two had slept together just a couple of times over the summer, so he put it out of his mind and allowed his ego to be stroked. He was once again Kimberly's everything—perhaps now more than ever.

Over the next couple of months, Powers and McGovern met with the San Diego assistant district attorney who was prosecuting the case against the Del Mar co-conspirators. They were able to convince the DA that Gunderson had been the brains behind the scam. Powers, they claimed, had been far too green at that point to lead such an operation. But the deal was truly sealed when Powers agreed to a plea bargain: he would testify against Gunderson and the Del Mar brokers; his testimony would cover the SURF IPO and several other questionable transactions.

However, Powers's plea bargain did not stipulate that he wouldn't serve time—after all, the tax evasion and money laundering charges were quite serious. Still, copping a plea was his best option, and there was a chance that he'd avoid prison. He just prayed that in the course of the investigation no one dug up any damning evidence against him—evidence relating to the deals he'd done at Pacific. Only time would tell.

In the meantime, he was free, and the trial was a long way off. Depositions on the charges, especially those involving offshore activity, would take a long time to complete. Until then, Powers decided, he was just going to take it easy and spend some of that money he'd "earned." After all he'd been through, he deserved it. Right?

4

Bringing Down the House:
Bear Raids and Short-Sale Scams

When an investor thinks that the price of a stock is about to drop, he or she may decide to take advantage of the situation by initiating a short-sell transaction through a brokerage (either physical or online). Here's how it works.

The brokerage loans the investor shares of the stock in question, taking the shares from its own inventory; alternatively, the brokerage may borrow the shares from another customer's margin account or from another brokerage. The investor then sells the shares. Later, the investor will be obliged to purchase the shares back and return them to the brokerage for the current market price. If the current market price is lower than the market price that was in effect the day the brokerage extended the loan of the shares, then the investor can pocket the profits—the difference between the two prices. If, however, the current market price is higher, then the investor has to "cover the short"—that is, the investor must buy the shares at the higher price and return them to the brokerage, absorbing the loss resulting from the price difference.

Not only is this technique used to make money in a market downturn, but it is also employed as a means of evaluating a stock's performance. If large quantities of a certain stock are being sold short, it indicates that investors are expecting its price to drop. Such indications can push the price of a stock down dramatically, which is why short-selling trends make pump-and-dump fraudsters very nervous.

But other fraudsters turn the strategy to their own advantage—short selling on insider knowledge or on downward price manipulation is yet another type of investment industry scam. One approach to it is called a "bear raid," which is a conspiracy to short sell specific securities in an effort to drive the price down (through a sell-side imbalance). The co-conspirators in the raid profit from their collective short positions. On October 28, 2002, the NASD busted just such a manipulation.

*   *   *

According to NASD records, the scam was inaugurated in early 1995. A small brokerage called Hanover Sterling and Company underwrote a group of 10 securities, all of which were microcaps—low-priced stocks issued by the smallest of companies. The microcap companies, each of which issued stock offerings of various sizes—ranging from 400,000 shares to one million shares—all went public between 1993 and 1994. NASD reported that Hanover, in typical boiler-room fashion, had attempted to pump and dump the stocks, but the scam never got off the ground.

Among those involved was John Fiero, who started his own firm, Fiero Brothers, in 1991 with $250,000. By 1995, the firm's capital had swollen to nearly $9 million. This spectacular increase was based entirely on John Fiero's personal trading activities—Fiero Brothers had no retail clientele, and John Fiero was the firm's only employee. Fiero was a veteran of the securities industry, having started out in the business in the early 1980s, and he knew that the world of penny-stock investing was rife with corruption. By the time he established Fiero Brothers, he'd seen it all. Fully aware that many bulletin board–market offerings were at best unstable and at worst fraudulent, he decided to become a short seller of penny stocks.

If he was to navigate the OTC markets successfully, Fiero needed a steady supply of information, so he got down to collecting this information—which he referred to as "intelligence"—by networking relentlessly with other industry players. While doing this, he met two particularly helpful sources, John Moran and Philip Gurian.

In 1995, Moran, an industry consultant, worked with Hanover Sterling bringing in underwriting clients. An acquaintance of his, Philip Gurian, introduced him to Fiero. Gurian had at one time been a licensed broker, but in 1991 the NASD had revoked his license for failing to pay a fine he had incurred over previous industry transgressions. Gurian spent much of his day at two firms, Falcon Trading Group and Sovereign Equity Management. Although he had no legal affiliation with either firm, he executed trades and answered phones. Moran later claimed that Glenn Vittor, president of record for both Falcon and Sovereign, was merely a rubber stamp for Philip Gurian.

This sets the stage for the bear raid. Hanover underwrites

microcap securities; Fiero sets himself up as a short seller; Fiero meets Gurian, who allegedly controls two brokerages; and, through Gurian, Fiero meets Moran, who transacts regular business with Hanover.

In early January 1995, a broker friend of Fiero's opened an account under the name of DiPrimo at a brokerage called A.T. Brod and Company. Another account was opened as well—a proprietary account at Falcon Trading Group. Both accounts took short positions in the Hanover issues. On January 11, 1995, the first trade was executed in the DiPrimo account: a short sale on three Hanover issues estimated at about $250,000. On January 17, the DiPrimo account again sold short on Hanover underwritten securities; there were six different issues involved, and this time the same six were shorted in the Falcon account (with the Falcon short sale carrying a market price tag of approximately $519,000).

The next day, the DiPrimo account sold short on two more Hanover issues. Falcon did the same, and it sold short on four others as well, increasing its short position in Hanover underwritten securities to $2 million. The conspiracy to create a sell-side imbalance was starting to become evident. The pressure was on Hanover, which, as underwriter, controlled substantial positions in the securities being shorted and stood to lose a great deal as the price of the stock declined.

Desperate to stop the bleeding, Hanover asked Moran for help. One of Moran's consulting clients, Sea Bright Foods, was supposed to be taken public by Hanover in early 1995; but, as Hanover pointed out to Moran, due to the downward pressure on its issues, it wouldn't be able to complete the Sea Bright offering. So Moran contacted John Fiero and asked him to act as "market maker" for the Hanover securities. A market maker is a brokerage or bank that agrees to buy or sell a certain security at a publicly quoted price; if the price is met, the market maker immediately buys or sells the security from its own accounts; market makers play an important role in keeping securities liquid. Moran was hoping that because Fiero was a renowned short seller, the fact that he'd signed on as one of Hanover's market makers would influence other short sellers to change their view of the securities. Between January 19 and 20, Fiero registered as market maker for all but one of the Hanover issues.

Moran continued his efforts to stabilize Hanover's issues by calling other well-known short sellers and urging them to change their positions. One call he placed was to Stephen Carlson, owner of Aspen Capital Group (a couple of years later, Carlson was barred from the industry for attempting to procure stock for a below-market price through "coercion" in 1994). The day Moran called, however, Carlson wasn't in, so he left a message in which he outlined his request. Moran expected to hear back from Carlson, but instead he got a call from Gurian. Carlson had relayed Moran's message to Gurian, and Gurian was calling to offer a suggestion on how to handle the situation. He told Moran that Hanover could make the short selling go away by transferring large blocks of its securities to the shorting firms to cover their positions at a profit. This way, the short sellers would make money and the negative pressure would be alleviated. Can anybody say "extortion!"

But Hanover wasn't interested in making deals with Carlson's firm, or any other firm, for that matter. Then, on January 20, on a CNBC broadcast, influential financial journalist Dan Dorfman cast serious doubts on Hanover's offerings, especially securities of Panax, a company that purported to be developing pharmaceuticals from medicinal plants. Panax had gone public on January 18 at $5 per share, and the price had immediately soared to $23. Dorfman maintained that the company had zero revenue, was losing money, and possessed no commercially usable products. He even quoted Carlson as saying that he'd been threatened by a Hanover executive and that the stock was worthless. On January 21, the short selling intensified, and Hanover was effectively coerced into negotiating with Gurian.

Between January 21 and 25, the short positions increased dramatically. Also, telephone records dating from this period show that Fiero, Carlson, Gurian, Moran, and Falcon were in constant communication; Fiero was speaking to people at Falcon about 20 times a day. As market maker for the Hanover offerings, Fiero should have kept his distance from the action, but by January 25, he'd amassed a short position in seven Hanover securities worth approximately $1.2 million. By the same date, Falcon had built a short position in the same seven securities valued at $2.9 million. Likewise, the DiPrimo account at A.T. Brod held a short position in the seven issues worth $1.8 million.

Through his network, Fiero learned about the deal going down between Carlson and Hanover, and he heard that Carlson would be brokering the Hanover securities. He immediately contacted Moran and convinced him that he, Fiero, should be the one to broker the block of securities Hanover was going to give in return for stopping the short selling. Fiero told Moran that he knew another market maker for Hanover securities at a firm called Mitchum Jones, and this market maker held the largest short position in those securities. Fiero assured Moran that once the shorts were covered by Hanover the activity would stop, and that those registered as market makers would "get off the box."

On January 26 and 27, Fiero Brothers purchased 974,000 shares, units, or warrants from Hanover for a total of about $12 million. This brought Fiero's discount—his profit—to $866,500. The securities purchased from Hanover matched the securities held in short positions at Falcon, in the DiPrimo account, and, of course, in the Fiero Brothers account. Fiero used a portion of the Hanover block to cover his own positions at the discount, pocketing roughly $568,000 in profits, and he sold the rest to his associates to cover theirs at a similar discount. Falcon profited to the tune of $694,000 after covering its short position, and the DiPrimo account realized a profit of $491,500. Not bad for just over two weeks' work. By the end of the trading day on January 27, all short positions in the three leader firms were flat or nearly flat—that is, they were covered. As per Fiero's agreement with Moran, both Fiero Brothers and Mitchum Jones withdrew as market makers in every Hanover security they had registered in. This marked the conclusion of a successful bear raid—or so Hanover thought.

But what Hanover didn't know was that the raiders were actually gearing up for a second and more intense stage of their attack. On January 30, the first trading day after the Hanover transaction, Fiero Brothers and its cohorts started short selling with a vengeance. Between January 30 and February 23, Fiero's short position in eight of Hanover's issues grew to $3.23 million. The DiPrimo account followed suit, establishing a position worth about $2.5 million by February 24. Falcon got back into the game, and by February 23 it had built a short position in nine Hanover securities worth over $7.5 million. The raiders were betting hard on these securities going under. There wouldn't be any block-trade bail-out this time.

Finally, like a gazelle taken down by lions, Hanover expired. On Friday, February 24, 1995, the brokerage went out of business. And it didn't die alone—on February 27, Hanover's clearing firm, Adler Coleman, was forced to shut down as well. The two-stage bear raid was over.

But the raid's second stage wasn't quite the success that it seemed. After the demise of Adler Coleman, the Securities Investor Protection Corporation (SIPC), an organization that insures customers of a brokerage against the brokerage's failure, stepped in. The SIPC proceeded to buy-in many short positions in Hanover securities, including Fiero's.

On October 28, 2002, after lengthy investigations and appeals on the part of the respondents in the case, a NASD hearing panel banned John Fiero from the NASD and fined him one million dollars for illegal short selling, extortion, and securities manipulation.

*   *   *

In 1995, the year the bear raid crushed Hanover and the popularity of the boiler rooms was at its peak, the FBI conducted a nationwide campaign to root out and convict the perpetrators of securities fraud. It was all part of the bureau's campaign to crack down on the growing trend of penny-stock manipulation. One of its targets was a notorious San Diego boiler-room kingpin named Melvin Lloyd Richards, who pushed worthless stocks through a series of chop-shop brokerages to the investing public. In the net it cast to ensnare Richards, the FBI also caught a broker named Amr "Anthony" Elgindy.

In 1988, at the age of 28, Elgindy dropped out of San Diego State University and joined a brokerage called Blinder Robinson, a classic boiler room. Shortly thereafter, Blinder clients started accusing the aggressive young broker of making unauthorized trades, misrepresenting facts, and trading excessively to maximize his commissions. Even Elgindy's mother found fault with his business conduct. In 1992, she charged that her son had executed unauthorized trades in her pension account, and the NASD arbitrated her a settlement of $32,000.

Elgindy's actions seemed to reflect the culture at Blinder Robinson, and by 1992 the firm was being called to account for its misdeeds. Under investigation by the SEC for securities manipulation and plagued with client lawsuits, Blinder filed for bankruptcy. This did not, however, thwart Elgindy's ambition, and he remained in the business, at one point working for a boutique brokerage called Thomas James. After a period of bouncing from firm to firm, Elgindy found a mentor in Melvin Richards. Their association led to Elgindy's 1995 arrest by the FBI. But Elgindy cut a deal with the feds. He agreed to wear a wire, and for 16 months he collected evidence against a number of securities fraudsters. He eventually testified in the Richards prosecution, and, according to the U.S. Attorney's Office, his testimony was largely responsible for sending Richards to prison.

During the time he worked as an FBI informant, Elgindy thought long and hard about the industry, gradually forming a new view of it. Instead of trying to get ahead by trading in clients' accounts or slinging worthless issues, he should exploit his knowledge of the liabilities and wrongdoings of various companies. In other words, it dawned on him that there was a lot more money to be made in short selling. With a renewed sense of purpose, Elgindy set up a website and a subscription-based newsletter to inform short sellers about companies that were going under and to warn investors about stock scam artists. Through this initiative—and, of course, through short selling on his own advice—Elgindy became rich. Very rich. He bought a mansion worth over $2 million and collected vehicles, including a Ferrari and a Humvee.

Elgindy's website grew steadily more popular, and his fiery diatribes on failing or fraudulent companies conferred on him the status of a celebrated gunslinger: he was the man who fearlessly confronted the forces of corruption and showed honest people how to make money in the process. It wasn't long before Elgindy was a nationally recognized short seller with a devout following. But with success came the inevitable criticism. The questions the skeptics raised most often were these: How did Elgindy know which companies were going under? What techniques did he use in making his short-sell recommendations? He was correct so often—there had to be an explanation. His critics started to wonder if Elgindy was in some way responsible for the demise of the companies he was shorting.

In fact, Elgindy did use some unorthodox techniques to gain access to inside information. On one occasion, he visited a Nevada-based petroleum clean-up company called SulphCo. Employing an alias, he informed SulphCo management that he was considering a $3 million investment in the company contingent upon a tour of the facilities and a review of the financial records. SulphCo's doors opened wide to receive him.

Upon his return from SulphCo, Elgindy posted his findings on his website. He reported that SulphCo's management and facilities were substandard and that company founder Rudy Gunnerman had a history of making unsuccessful product offerings. In his scathing and colorful style, Elgindy trashed SulphCo so viciously that Gunnerman brought a lawsuit against him, charging him with fraud. However, many of Elgindy's allegations appeared to have some foundation, especially after the SEC issued a report accusing SulphCo of violating securities laws. But how had Elgindy determined that SulphCo had all these problems on the basis of a single visit?

Elgindy's critics were becoming more vocal. They started to ask whether the short-selling guru had informants in the SEC. They wanted to know whether the FBI was feeding him tips in exchange for information on illegal activities within the industry. Then Elgindy came under the scrutiny of authorities investigating aspects of the September 11, 2001 attacks on the World Trade Center and the Pentagon. He'd attracted their attention by donating funds to Muslim refugees in Kosovo and by purchasing a condo in Lebanon.

In June 2002, federal prosecutors indicted Elgindy and four others—Troy Peters, Derrick Cleveland, Jeff Royer, and Lynn Wingate—for conspiring to drive down the stock price of certain companies and shorting the stock for a profit. As it turned out, Cleveland was a subscriber to Elgindy's website and newsletter; Royer was an FBI agent and a friend of Cleveland's; and Wingate, herself an FBI agent, was Royer's girlfriend. The prosecutors alleged that Cleveland paid Royer and Wingate for FBI insider information on the companies in question and then passed it on to Elgindy, who used it to target the companies on his site. At last, Elgindy's scamming days were over. He was charged with a variety of offenses, including racketeering, extortion, stock manipulation, and misusing classified government information.

*   *   *

Deciding to engage in short selling is as serious an investment decision as any other. The short-selling investor can make money on the downside of a security; and in the wild world penny stocks, short sellers can realize enormous gains. However, collusive short selling is a crime. The practice can kill microcap companies, bankrupt small brokerages, and, worst of all, ruin honest investors who have purchased shares of the companies being shorted. Needless to say, the authorities take this type of activity very seriously.

5

A Den of Thieves

EXPOSÉ

Mike Flannigan sat at his mahogany desk gazing at his computer screen. Stock prices flickered in apparently random patterns on the grid before him. He knew all too well, however, that patterns in this business were seldom random, especially when it came to penny stocks.

The last firm Flannigan had worked for had been driven into the ground by the unethical practices of its owners and employees—commission skimming, sexual harassment, and the like. When that chop shop had shut down, he'd checked out what the wire houses had to offer. It took some convincing, but the prestigious Solomon Lynch in San Diego had finally taken him on. But at Solomon Lynch, Flannigan had learned that even the illustrious houses of high finance practiced their own brand of bullshit.

Solomon Lynch's brokers were pressured to push house products on their clients—primarily mutual funds. Of course, the firm offered no financial incentives to brokers who sold these products, but the pressure was definitely on. Still, what bugged Flannigan most about working at Solomon Lynch was the atmosphere. It was common knowledge that in any brokerage, most new brokers—and many of the more experienced ones—knew little about finance. They were salespeople first and foremost. At Solomon Lynch, this was particularly true. Flannigan's work mates had no energy, no aggression. They were just a bunch of pretentious rich kids Solomon Lynch had hired to bring in the investment dollars of their wealthy friends and families.

All these novice brokers dressed well, carried cell phones, and passed out business cards, but the accounts they opened were for clients within that small circle of wealthy connections. They strutted around like pros at the top of their game, but they were nothing more than what the chop-shop guys called "pikers"—they were poseurs, losers. Their days were spent clicking away at their computers, reading the *Wall Street Journal*, and making a few phone calls (no more than 50 a day). Such an obvious lack of drive irritated Flannigan deeply. It made him crazy when the bespectacled Christian conservative at the desk next to his berated him for his phone technique or the profane language he used when talking to his buddies who still toiled at the smaller firms. This place was sucking the life out of him!

Thoughts like these ran through Flannigan's head as he sat staring at his computer screen. The phone rang. "Hey, Mike, how's it going?" It was Tony Fiarello, a senior broker Flannigan had worked with when he put in some rookie time at Sloan Michaels. Fiarello was a large man with a pleasant demeanor and a winning smile. He was also one of the most adept salesmen

Flannigan knew. Fiarello was greedy, but so was everyone else who survived in the business—in wire houses and boiler rooms alike. In fact, greed was considered a positive attribute. Greed gave you the drive to generate money, and money made the world go round.

Fiarello explained to his former cohort that after he left Sloan Michaels, he'd worked for various brokerages. He had recently joined some old friends at a firm called Chicago Capital. He'd managed to convince them that they should open a branch office out here in San Diego; after some negotiating, they had agreed to lend Fiarello their name, trading desk, and clearing house. The pay-out would be 80 percent to the brokers, and 20 percent to Chicago Capital. It seemed like a pretty good deal all around.

Then Fiarello got to the point of his call. He wanted to invite Flannigan to be a part of the broker team he was putting together. He couldn't have got to Flannigan at a better moment. The wire house life was stable, but Flannigan had recently come to the realization that he'd lose his mind if he had to spend the rest of his working life planning retirements and rolling over IRAs. After all, he was a stockbroker, not a fucking banker! Telling Fiarello that he'd give the idea some serious thought, he hung up the phone.

Pondering the numbers Fiarello had laid out for him, it suddenly occurred to him that this was going to be his last day at Solomon Lynch. Leaving wouldn't be so hard—he was getting pretty used to the procedure. First, he opened his briefcase and removed all unnecessary brochures and documents. Next, he filled his briefcase with the handwritten lead cards he had collected over the eight months he'd spent at the wire house.

Brokers were actually expected to enter all of their leads into the wire house database, but Flannigan was far too savvy at this point in his career to have even considered it. He recorded his leads the old-fashioned way, on oversized note cards, listing all pertinent information about his prospects.

To complete his preparations for departure, Flannigan tore off a big stack of uncalled numbers from Solomon Lynch's lead source sheets and stashed them in his briefcase as well. Later that night, he'd go to Kinkos and copy everything. Tossing his sports coat over his shoulder, he switched off his monitor. On his way down the hall, he stuck his head into his sales manager's office and informed him that he was off to meet an important prospect. The manager, ear glued to his telephone receiver, gave him a hearty thumbs-up.

In fact, Flannigan was going to the address he had scratched on a yellow Post-It, now crumpled in his sweaty hand. It was the address of Chicago Capital. He wanted to check out the facilities Fiarello had procured for the branch office and meet the other brokers on the team.

The prospect of change was stimulating to Flannigan, who just that morning had felt caught in a low-energy rut. What he was contemplating was not out of the ordinary, however—people were always changing jobs in this business, especially those who worked in the boutique brokerages. Chicago Capital would be Flannigan's fourth firm in just three years, but that was all part of the excitement. It was one big gamble, and only those who could seize risky opportunities without hesitation would win.

Pulling his beat-up Oldsmobile into the parking lot of the building that housed Chicago Capital, Flannigan noticed that the edifice was two stories high, modern, and unassuming. He stepped out of the car and took a moment to ready himself for his meeting with Fiarello. Fiarello, he knew, needed brokers who could push whatever crap he would be getting his hands on in the course of his "investment banking" deals. For his part, Flannigan didn't much care what he had to do as long as the money was good.

Chicago Capital was located on the second floor. Mike made his way up the stairs leading from the lobby and walked down the hall towards Chicago's open door. Behind the reception desk sat a very attractive sandy-haired girl of about 25 wearing a revealing black top. She didn't notice him at first. Clearing his throat, he startled her. "Hello!" she said in a sweet voice. Flannigan introduced himself, said he had a meeting with Tony Fiarello, and announced that he'd probably be working there by the end of the week. As she picked up her phone to buzz Fiarello, she shot him a sexy sideways glance and a smile. "Good," she said.

A door behind the reception desk swung open, and Fiarello came barreling out. He greeted Flannigan with a solid handshake and a slap on the back and gestured for him to follow. As they moved further into the suite, Flannigan saw that (aside from the reception area) Chicago Capital was comprised of one large room, furnished with a couple of desks, and two small offices opening off it. The doors to these offices, one of which was Fiarello's, stood open. In the second office, he could see a short, dark-haired man in a black golf shirt pacing and talking into a headset receiver. Fiarello explained to Flannigan that the man was his partner, Dennis Morales.

At one of the desks in the main room sat a tall, lanky fellow whose strawlike hair was cut in bushy mop, seventies style. Sporting white pants, a Hawaiian shirt, and rose-tinted shades, he talked on the phone, his sandal-clad feet resting on the desktop. "That's Otis," explained Fiarello. "He's one of the best fucking closers in the business." Flannigan would later find out that this was, in fact, an understatement. Otis Wiley had a knack for lulling his unfortunate clients into a false sense of security. His tone quietly confident, his voice hypnotizing, he'd persuade them to accept his recommendations.

Flannigan's excitement mounted. Here, he was sure, he could learn how to make a lot of cash. Fiarello invited him into his office to discuss the situation. Once they were seated, he got straight to the point. Through some of his business connections, he said, he was able to strike extremely lucrative deals in the form of house stocks or private placements. Either way, he would be able to pay Flannigan on a per-share-sold basis or, in some cases, on a percentage basis. The people at Chicago Capital's Chicago headquarters would take 20 percent of all commissions, while the San Diego branch team would get 80 percent. Then Fiarello explained that since he, Flannigan, wasn't a partner, he would receive a 50 percent pay-out and the branch would keep the other 30 percent. He'd neglected to mention this last piece of information in their initial conversation. It was a tremendous improvement on the 20 percent pay-out Flannigan was getting from Solomon Lynch.

Fiarello went on to say that everyone at Chicago (San Diego) was family, and that he already considered Flannigan a son. This firm, he insisted, was a place where loyalty meant something, and where they could all work together as an independent team to make some real money. Pep talks like this failed to inspire Flannigan, who had been around the block a few times. Still, the idea of working in a casual yet energized environment was very enticing to him. By the end of their conversation, he'd agreed to join Fiarello's team. An ecstatic Fiarello reached into his desk drawer and pulled out a large bottle of single malt scotch. He slammed it down on the desk between them, grabbed two tumblers from another drawer, and poured out the golden liquid. They toasted their new association.

Returning to the main room, Fiarello and Flannigan went over to the empty desk next to Wiley's. "This one's yours, buddy," said Fiarello . Without looking up from the paperwork he was now engaged in, Wiley said, "What's up, man?" Fiarello made the introductions. Flannigan briefly explained that he was moving over from Solomon Lynch and he'd be starting Monday. Wiley suggested that they all go out and celebrate Flannigan's hiring.

This sounded good to Fiarello. He called to Morales, telling him to come and meet the new guy and head out with them for a drink. Morales emerged from his office, his curly black hair stuck to his sweaty forehead. He extended his pudgy hand, gave Flannigan's a shake, and said, "How ya do'n Mike? Dennis Morales. Where we go'n?" His accent was definitely East Coast, but Flannigan couldn't quite place it. Fiarello proposed they hit The Florentine, and all agreed.

Flannigan reflected on the fact that he could consign almost all the brokers he encountered to one of two categories: the fat ones, addicted to steak and cigars; and the skinny ones, addicted to booze and drugs. (All brokers chain-smoked cigarettes.) He put Fiarello and Morales in the first category, Wiley in the second.

Just before they left the office in pursuit of liquid refreshment, Wiley picked up the phone. He wanted to ask a couple of his

buddies who worked at a brokerage across town to meet them—
"Justin and Alejandro are coming too." Rolling his eyes, Fiarello
said to Flannigan, "You'll love these guys, Mike. They're wack
jobs." Following his new crew out onto the street, Flannigan felt
great. This was exactly where he wanted to be—where the
money was. He was more than ready to share the perks. He'd
drink the scotch, smoke the cigars, eat at the city's finest restaurants, and he'd enjoy every minute of it.

As they piled into Fiarello's white Range Rover, Wiley cut in
front of Morales and claimed the front passenger seat. Morales
may have had an office to himself, but there was no other
evidence of his seniority. On the way to The Florentine, Wiley
regaled them all with a memorable tale of business-related
pillage and plunder. He and a client of his, a young television
producer, had traveled to Las Vegas together and rented a luxu-
rious hotel suite. While gambling at a casino, they met two
women and lured them back to the suite with the promise of
some high-grade coke. But after indulging in the blow and
downing a few drinks, Wiley and the producer decided that
they needed more than two women to make things interesting.
They cooked up a twisted sexual scheme, and Wiley went down
to the strip to corral a few willing prostitutes.

It only took him a few minutes to spot and approach a likely
candidate—a busty blond in a tight red skirt and heels. Wiley
wasn't one to mince words. He asked her if she was a prostitute.
When she told him she was, he explained that he and his friend
were looking for five women who were willing to do "everything."
The hooker volunteered to round up four of her friends and
quoted him a price of $500 apiece. They would agree to perform
the necessary acts, she assured him, especially if good drugs

were offered to sweeten the deal. Wiley laughed, promised good money and good drugs, and made sure that the hooker had committed the suite number to memory.

Returning to the suite, he bragged to the producer about how successful his mission had been. The producer rewarded him with a thick, dusty line. Wiley took the line down in one emphatic snort, tilted his head back, and drew the remnants of the drug deep into his sinuses. He felt the effects instantly, letting out a whoop. Shortly afterwards, there was a knock at the door. The producer answered it, and five sultry hookers filed into the room.

There were three blonds, one with dark roots just starting to show, and two brunettes, one of whom looked Latina. The producer ushered them into the living room of the suite, where Wiley and the two women they'd picked up at the casino sat at a table, busily chatting and snorting. Wiley was chopping up lines as fast as the ladies could do them. They greeted the new arrivals with enthusiastic applause, and the producer introduced them as, "our willing playthings for tonight's festivities!"

Before those festivities got underway, however, Wiley and the producer wanted to explain to the women what was expected of them. Wiley had them all sit on a semicircular couch, and then he dumped out another plastic sack of white powder on the glass coffee table in front of them. He set up more lines, and the hookers spent about 20 minutes diving nose-first into the table. When everyone seemed momentarily satisfied, enjoying the buzz, Wiley stood, raised his glass of scotch, and proposed a toast to the producer—his friend and his best client—"without whom this night would not have been possible." Then he explained their idea. The hookers were compliant, but the two casino ladies opted to watch; taking more coke with them, they retreated to a safe distance.

Getting up from the couch, the hookers went around behind it and bent over the back, their bellies pressed against the seat cushions. Wiley and the producer approached each woman from the rear, lifted her skirt, and removed her panties. They proceeded to sodomize them in succession. Explained Wiley, "They didn't want us to use the same rubber, though, so we had to keep switching them. There were rubbers flying everywhere!"

In the Range Rover, passengers and pilot were in an uproar over this tale. They thought it was hilarious. And Flannigan again congratulated himself on making an inspired career decision. He smiled to think of all the mayhem the money he was about to earn could buy him.

As they pulled up to the building where The Florentine was located, Wiley saw Alejandro's black Mercedes parked at the curb. The Florentine was a bar-restaurant located on the building's top floor. Stepping out of the elevator and surveying the establishment—a rooftop terrace with a great view and linen-covered, candlelit tables—Flannigan was duly impressed. This was a really nice place. While he was no rookie, Flannigan was still a mid-level broker, and he had little experience with watering holes of this caliber. He hadn't yet had a $20,000 month; his personal best was $11,000, and he'd only done it once. His monthly average at that point was $3,000 to $4,000.

Back in their Sloan Michaels days, Flannigan recalled, Fiarello had once received a bimonthly paycheck of $30,000. Flannigan knew that he was doing pretty well for a guy from a blue-collar background with not much more than a high school education, but he was also aware that his drinking companions for that evening were in a whole other league. They made and spent huge quantities of cash, and because of it they exuded power.

Many terrace tables had already been claimed by a variety of patrons. There were conservative-looking businessmen taking the edge off their day and discussing their latest endeavors; young couples on special dates; and several well-heeled middle-aged couples. The Chicago Capital crew stuck out like sore thumbs—except, ironically, for Flannigan, who was still dressed in his Solomon Lynch suit-and-tie uniform.

Wiley asked the dapper maitre d' if Justin and Alejandro had already been seated. They had. The maitre d' led them to a table in the far corner of the terrace, where Justin and Alejandro sat with several empty shot glasses ranged before them. They had clearly wasted no time. They gave the Chicago Capital crew an uproarious greeting, disrupting conversations at the surrounding tables. The new arrivals, except for Flannigan, boisterously returned the greeting—about as inconspicuous as a herd of pink rhinos in a shopping mall. All of these guys were loud and disrespectful. They felt entitled to be.

Everyone was hungry, so they decided to order dinner. One advantage to hanging with the loud crowd, Flannigan realized, was that your food came fast. Fiarello and Morales had chosen substantial meat dishes; the rest picked at a variety of appetizers, washing the food down with liberal amounts of scotch. The two carnivores barely looked up from their plates as they devoured their steak and potatoes. Flannigan's initial pleasure at being indoctrinated into the good life was now mingled with disgust. The noise and the gorging had gotten to him, but he didn't want to think about it, so he just kept drinking. By the time everyone was ready to leave, he was pissed. So were Wiley, Alejandro, and Justin, who had become even more obnoxious.

Fiarello whipped out a gold credit card and settled the check. As they rolled out of The Florentine—much to the relief of the staff and the other patrons—they launched into a loud discussion about whether they should move the party to a strip club. Justin knew of a place, Déjà Vu, that hired girls who could be persuaded to attend private parties after work—at Wiley's apartment, perhaps?

Suddenly, there was a resounding crash, then screaming and raised voices. Drunken Alejandro, who had been trailing a few paces behind the group, was now lying face-down across a table, struggling to get back on his feet. Beside him lay another table, knocked onto its side. Broken china and glass, silverware, and bits of food were scattered everywhere. The sloshed broker had tripped and crashed into the first table, knocking it and an elderly woman to the ground. Lurching away from that disaster, he'd collided with the second table, diving onto it face first and sending food, beverages, and place settings flying in all directions.

Justin and Wiley roared with laughter at the sight, but Fiarello and Morales knew that Alejandro had crossed the line. They rushed over to the floundering broker and, each seizing an arm, they hauled him up. All the while, they apologized profusely to the flabbergasted and indignant diners Alejandro had landed upon. Alejandro was a mess—he was covered in food and soaked with wine, coffee, and water. A flower from a table arrangement was plastered to his wet cheek.

As they fled to the elevators, dragging Alejandro along with them, they were pursued by the distraught maitre d', who informed them that they would be charged for the damage. Furthermore, if they ever dared to darken The Florentine's door again, he'd call the police. Flannigan was surprised that the police hadn't been summoned already.

All six brokers, disheveled and reeking of alcohol, piled into the elevator. The elevator stopped to take on two more passengers, a middle-aged man and his young son. Although the man held his son in front of him and stared straight ahead, Justin decided to interpret his attitude as disrespectful. He started shouting that he didn't like to be ignored and he was going to teach the guy some manners by kicking his ass right there, in front of his son. Fiarello managed to calm him down a bit, but as they got off the elevator, Justin yelled at the man, "I make more money in one month than you do in an entire year!"

And that's the crux of it all. There is a pervasive attitude in the brokerage business that the amount of respect you deserve corresponds directly to the amount of money you make. Money equals respect, and vice versa. Rookies who pound the phones for 15 hours a day are indoctrinated with this attitude. Senior brokers scream at them that they're worthless, and their meager paychecks reflect their worthlessness. In a culture of greed, it's just the way things are. It's the law of the jungle. And many young, poorly educated brokers believe that for them, there's no way out of the jungle. The only thing they're good at is selling—opening accounts, setting up shady deals, pumping and dumping, chasing the money.

The Chicago crew, Justin, and Alejandro reconvened beside Fiarello's Range Rover. Fiarello and Morales wanted to get home to their families and, in any case, they'd had enough for one night. Wiley and Justin wanted to head over to Déjà Vu.

Flannigan wasn't sure what he wanted to do, and Alejandro could barely stand up. In the end, the family men went home, Justin took Alejandro home, and Wiley and Flannigan made their way to the strip club. Justin would catch up with them later. It crossed Flannigan's mind that he still hadn't gone to Kinko's to copy his Solomon Lynch leads. He'd have to take care of it the next morning—after all, he was resigning from the wire house and getting back into the belly of the beast, and he still had celebrating to do!

The San Diego branch of Chicago Capital was a partnership between Fiarello, Morales, and Wiley. Fiarello claimed 50 percent of the revenue; Morales and Wiley each took 25 percent. But all of the branch's trades had to go through Morales, because he was the only one with a clean license. The licenses of Fiarello and Wiley had been temporarily suspended for various and separate violations of NASD rules—most of them related to making unauthorized trades. In addition, Fiarello was being investigated for selling unregistered stocks before he joined Sloan Michaels.

Chicago Capital's head office had only agreed to allow Fiarello to open the West Coast branch on the condition that he perform no trades himself. He'd met that condition by recruiting Morales, and now he had Flannigan, whose license was also clean. Fiarello would be relying on Flannigan to put through trades that he and Wiley were not permitted to touch. In other words, he'd hired Flannigan to exploit his good name.

Just before he'd snared Flannigan, a new deal had landed on Fiarello's plate. Chicago's head office had brought him an investment banking deal involving a company called Global Security Systems (GLSI). GLSI was just a patched-together security company designed to capitalize on the fear engendered by 9/11. It had little in the way of operations, but Fiarello thought he might be able to make some good money on its IPO.

He had teleconferenced in on a few of the meetings between Chicago Capital's head office and the CEO of GLSI. When he found out that he would be paid in both cash and stock, he became eager to put a team together and get the IPO moving. Fiarello brought Morales in first. Dennis Morales was not a very forceful person, which meant that he wouldn't interfere with the process too much, and he also had a decent list of client leads. He could place a lot of shares. Wiley came next. Tony had known Otis Wiley for about five years. In San Diego's relatively small brokerage circles, their paths had crossed and recrossed. Fiarello wasn't concerned that Wiley was still under suspension for some bullshit he'd been involved in a year earlier, because he had Morales to front for them, and he knew that Wiley could get the job done.

Fiarello had chosen Flannigan to round out the team, despite his limited experience, because he needed to beef up his front line of clean licensed brokers. Besides, he genuinely liked the guy. They came from similar backgrounds. He also felt that Flannigan had the potential to be a good salesman, and he enjoyed the prospect of grooming him for the business.

On Monday, Flannigan reported for his first day of work at Chicago Capital. Fiarello called everyone into his office and filled them in on the GLSI deal. He told his brokers that they would be getting paid on a per-share-sold basis—a buck a share. If they sold 20,000 shares, they would get $20,000. Simple as that. He also informed the team that if they collectively sold 100,000 shares by Friday, he would take them to Vegas, all expenses paid. Flannigan was psyched. He resolved to work harder than he'd ever worked before.

They all pushed hard the entire week, unaware that Fiarello had already bought their tickets to Vegas. He knew they'd be raking it in on this deal; besides, he was putting the whole excursion on the corporate card, which meant that it would go on the books as an expense, and Morales and Wiley would thus be sharing the tab. The bit about the 100,000 shares was simply intended to keep them all motivated through the week. Friday came at last, and at the close of the market Fiarello announced that they'd met their mark. They'd be flying to Las Vegas that night. Justin, Alejandro, and an old friend of Fiarello's called Damien—because, Fiarello joked, he was the devil incarnate—would be joining them. Flannigan had forgotten whatever misgivings had begun to creep up on him during the Florentine fiasco. He was on a victory high, and he was in the mood for adventure. He looked forward to partying with this rowdy bunch and creating some stories of his own.

Of course, the drinking began on the plane. At the Las Vegas air terminal, the limousine Fiarello had ordered was waiting for them, its wet bar well stocked. As they settled back on the plush seats, drinks in hand, the limo pulled away from the terminal and glided towards town and their hotel—the Mirage, right on the strip. Reaching into the inside pocket of his black leather jacket, Wiley produced a silver cigarette box. From it he took a tightly rolled joint. Lighting up, he passed the joint to Justin, who was sitting beside him.

Fiarello and Morales spurned the weed—Cuban cigars were more their style. Justin pulled out a travel-size Advil bottle and shook several pills into his palm. "Anyone for E?" he asked.

Flannigan had never tried Ecstasy before, but he helped himself, figuring it would be a fitting way to start things off. Justin, Alejandro, and Wiley all partook as well. Cracking open a Heineken, Flannigan used it to wash down the E. The revelers raised their assorted bottles and glasses and toasted Vegas. Now the party was really under way.

The limo cruised slowly down the congested strip, passing all sorts of oddities: pirate ships doing battle, giant rollercoasters, erupting volcanoes. Vast hotels towered above them and enormous flashing signs and video screens blared their hedonistic messages into the night. They rolled into the Mirage's circular driveway and came to a smooth stop. As they exited the limo, a cloud of smoke billowed out with them. Fortunately, the aroma of Cuban stogies had all but obliterated the smell of the marijuana. Flannigan had heard that dope smoking was a no-tolerance felony in Nevada because the casino operators wanted people to be in the casinos losing money, not stoned, holed up in their rooms, ordering from room service. But who knew whether this was true? All Flannigan knew was that he was high.

Fiarello sent the limo driver back to the airport to pick up Damien, who was arriving from Boston, and they entered the Mirage's opulent lobby to check in. Everybody had his own room, and it all went on Fiarello's card. Fiarello and Morales, the relatively subdued family men, had wisely reserved rooms on different floors from the others. Flannigan and the rest of the crew were not only on the same floor, but they were also in the same corridor—all set for the never-ending party.

Entering his well-appointed room, Flannigan tossed his duffel bag onto the king-size bed and went into the bathroom.

He'd just made himself comfortable on the oversized porcelain bowl when the bedside phone rang. He jumped up and shuffled awkwardly across the white carpet, his pants around his ankles, and scooped up the receiver, cutting off the shrill ring.

"Hello!" he shouted breathlessly into the mouthpiece.

"Hey dude!" It was Justin. "What are you doing?"

"I'm taking a shit. What's up?"

Justin told him that everyone was meeting in the sports bar downstairs in five minutes. He also mentioned that the E should be kicking in about now. Back on the bowl, Flannigan laughed out loud, his voice echoing around the large tiled bathroom. He could sense the room breathing—just slightly. Justin was right. It was E time.

He was drinking shots of Jack Daniels with his floor buddies in the sports bar, gazing at a seemingly endless succession of horse races on a series of wall-mounted TV screens, when Fiarello, Morales, and Damien walked in. Damien was a strange-looking fellow. He stood well over six feet tall, but he was exceedingly thin and very pale. His black hair was cut short, and he was wearing an Armani suit. He had an air of competence and restraint, like a high-powered investment banker. But as the night wore on, his behavior would begin to belie his appearance.

They were now a group of seven. For the next hour, they remained in the sports bar, slouching in comfortable leather club chairs, betting on the televised races, and drinking heavily. Fiarello, Morales, and Damien puffed away on Cubans, telling stories of their early days in the business and assuring Flannigan that before too long he'd be making more money than all of them combined. The booze and the E worked their magic, and Flannigan's head filled with fantasies of wealth and power.

Then it was time to go casino hopping. Wiley and Justin installed themselves at the card tables, slurping down the free drinks, making passes at cocktail waitresses, and losing hundreds of dollars. Fiarello and Morales stuck to craps, smoked like chimneys, and bet thousands of dollars on each roll of the dice. Flannigan, Damien, and Alejandro hung out at the bar. Every now and then, Fiarello would come over to Flannigan and slip him a couple of hundred dollars in chips, encouraging him to have fun and play some cards. The still sensible Flannigan pocketed the chips and continued drinking. When the gamblers were burnt out, the team regrouped and got set to embark on a tour of the strip clubs. This is what Flannigan had been waiting for. He cashed in his chips and stuffed the money into his pocket.

As a Vegas regular, Fiarello knew where to find strippers who would go as far as you wanted, depending on how much you were willing to spend. Shortly after they'd quit the casino, the seven partyers were drinking beer from their stage-side seats at a popular peeler joint off the strip. The girls here were phenomenally attractive. And Flannigan found some of their pole moves simply astounding.

Fiarello asked Flannigan which girl he liked, his breath reeking of cigars and alcohol. He explained that these girls were much more than dancers and declared that he was happy to treat his protégé to some of their expert attention. So Flannigan selected a petite blond, and Fiarello waved her over. The music was too loud for Flannigan to hear what the big man was saying to the girl, but he saw him press two hundred-dollar bills into her hand. She nodded, gave Fiarello a knowing smile, and came over to where Flannigan was sitting. Reaching out, the blond took the young broker by the hand and led him into the "VIP room"—a dark, curtained-off enclosure furnished with a leather couch.

Flannigan had been to his share of strip clubs back east, before he'd come out to the West Coast, but he'd never experienced anything like this. The stripper gave him a lap dance, then she told him that his boss had paid for a little something extra. For the next 10 minutes, she blew Flannigan away. He emerged from the VIP room with an enormous smile on his face. "They don't do that at the wire houses, do they buddy!" Fiarello shouted to him from across the club.

Young strippers were fawning all over Fiarello, despite the fact that he was far older than they were, overweight, and smoking a stinking cigar. "If you have enough money, anything goes," thought Flannigan. He saw Morales sitting alone at the bar. Once again, Alejandro had gotten pissed; the bouncers had thrown him out, but not before he'd vomited on the floor. Wiley, Justin, and Damien had left with some off-duty dancers. Flannigan cabbed it back to the Mirage with Morales and Fiarello—all three were ready to crash.

At breakfast the next morning—over Bloody Marys and Mimosas—Wiley and Justin (Damien never made it to breakfast) told the rest of the group what had happened to them. Three of the strippers at the club had been impressed with the amount of money that Wiley had been shelling out. One asked him if he was interested in a lap dance or a tryst in the VIP room, and he told her that he was looking for a much bigger party than that. She went off to see if two of her friends wanted to join them. A little while later, at the end of the peelers' shift, the six of them hailed a cab and headed out to do some drug shopping.

At the home of one of the girls' ex-boyfriends, they had purchased some coke. Wiley described the scene. The girl had called ahead and told the dealer what they wanted. She and Wiley went into the apartment while the others waited for them outside the complex. Staggering drunk and high on E, Wiley barely understood what was happening. The girl knocked on the dealer's door, and he responded almost immediately. He was pissed off to see Wiley at his door. Making sure that his handgun, which was jammed into his belt, was clearly visible, he asked the girl if Wiley was her new man. Wiley wanted to get out of there, but before he could get it together to bolt, the pusher had disappeared into the apartment and returned with a brown-paper sandwich bag. Without even looking inside the bag, Wiley thrust $500 at the dealer and made for the exit.

Now the partiers had eight grams of coke and six hits of Ecstasy. They each popped an E pill and braced themselves for a wild ride. Back in Justin's room at the Mirage, they dumped the coke out on a table and started doing lines. Damien went at it with a vengeance. To the breakfast group, Wiley commented, "I don't even think he gave a shit about the chicks!"

The E was taking hold. Wiley was making out with the drug dealer's ex, and Justin was feeling fine—he was sprawled on a velvet sofa with the other two peelers. Damien just kept blasting line after line. Every once in awhile, one of the girls would disentangle herself, go over to the table where Damien sat alone, and help herself to a line or two. Damien slowed down slightly, and in the intervals between lines he stared blankly into space. Justin and Wiley maintained their heavy buzz by drinking shots of Jack Daniels. Finally, however, Wiley's body rebelled, and he barricaded himself in the bathroom for a three-hour vomiting session.

As for Justin, he now had three hot chicks to contend with, but he was no longer up for it—literally. The coke and booze had taken their toll. All he could do was lie back and watch the girls engage in a little lesbian action. Damien, hoping to be the sole audience member for a live sex show, sat slumped in a corner, waiting to be entertained. The girls tried to revive Justin's faded glory, but to no avail. Exhausted, he passed out on the sofa.

At this point, Damien revived somewhat. Deprived of a sex show, he opted for the do-it-yourself approach. He pulled his manhood from his liquor-stained pants and, with a demonic laugh, attempted to masturbate. The girls were repelled by this and, scooping up the remaining drugs, they beat a hasty retreat. Damien's insane laughter echoed in their ears as they fled down the corridor.

The breakfast group was laughing so hard at this tale of debauchery that tears rolled down their faces. This was their definition of a good time.

Good time or not, when they all got back to the office on Monday morning, it was business as usual. Flannigan made over 500 calls that day, and he opened three accounts. Somehow, the trip to Vegas had inspired him to work harder than ever. And this was exactly what Fiarello had been banking on. The offices of Chicago Capital hummed for the next week as the brokers continued to sell GLSI stock like it was going out of style. Flannigan felt like he was holding a winning lottery ticket.

With every new account he opened, with every block of shares he sold, Flannigan updated the rip tally he kept on a small piece of paper taped to his desk. By the end of the week, he'd calculated that he alone, the low guy on the totem pole, would be pulling in 10 grand from the GLSI IPO. Then one day, about a week after the Vegas trip, Fiarello called a meeting to announce that the "scorecard"—the commission figures—had arrived from the head office. He had taken the liberty of highlighting his own sales. Passing the scorecard and a highlighter to Wiley, he asked him to mark his sales. Wiley dragged the highlighter across the printout. By the time the printout made it around to Flannigan, most of the sales figures had been claimed. Wiley and Morales were arguing over a couple of items on the list, and they also started accusing Fiarello of taking credit for some of their sales.

When the melee was over, Flannigan walked away with $3,000—a far cry from the 10 large he'd been expecting. But he'd learned a valuable lesson. Loyalty, friendship, and honor meant nothing in the chop-shop world. The buddies he'd made during the romp in Vegas, his Chicago Capital "family" members, were not what they seemed. They were his opponents in a dirty game, a game without rules. The bottom line for them was money. Nothing else mattered in the end. Flannigan began to think long and hard about where he was and what he was doing there.

6

Cyberscams and
Other Forms of Fraud

It's early evening. Wayne Johnson, the owner of a local pool-cleaning supply store, finishes his dinner and retires to his home office to begin his nightly ritual of surfing the Web. He enjoys educating himself about investment strategies and researching ways to earn extra income. Occasionally, he engages in a fantasy of finding a stock that will make him a rich man.

In the past, he has tried working with stockbrokers at independent brokerages, but the stocks they tout always seem to lose him money. He has become fed up with their incessant phone calls and their offhand attitude towards his losses. He hates their glib jokes and bullying sales tactics. These days, he's taking matters into his own hands and picking his own investment opportunities. Tonight he plans to make his usual rounds of message boards and chat rooms where he can exchange tips and discuss ideas with like-minded individuals. Once in awhile, someone will suggest a useful website, and he'll pursue his investigation there. It's all far less stressful than dealing with a high-pressure, loudmouth broker.

First, Johnson signs onto his e-mail account to pick up his messages and clear out any junk mail that has accumulated. A particular subject line catches his attention. It's about increasing one's investment *"tenfold!"* Sounds good to Johnson. The message contains a brief description of a company called Spectrum Brands Corporation, which is listed on the OTC Bulletin Board. Spectrum is e-mailing him to let him know that it has obtained exclusive distribution rights to a device called the DeGERMinator. This device, the message claims, can kill anthrax in less than five seconds! Johnson has been looking for just such an opportunity. As a matter of fact, not long after the 9/11 attacks, he had predicted to his wife that any company selling anti-terrorist products would be minting money in the next couple of years.

Before he's even finished reading the message, Johnson clicks on the link to the company's website. There he browses through several promising press releases and learns that Spectrum is actually the holding company for a subsidiary called Spectrum Homeland Security Services. The company is involved in the development and distribution of products that fight bio and cyber terrorism. The distribution contract for the DeGERMINator is the first the company has signed. Johnson is convinced that this is one of those "ground-floor opportunities" he has heard so much about.

Using ultraviolet light, the DeGERMINator kills all bacteria and virus strains and, to top it off, it's handheld. Johnson notices a link on the site to his local television station—it's an interview with the CEO of the company that developed the product, a Mr. Jon Cooper. In the interview, Cooper confirms the efficacy of the DeGERMINator and its ability to kill anthrax. Johnson is getting very excited. His next step is to check out the chart.

He logs on to one of the financial sites he uses to pull up charts on perspective stock purchases and types in the ticker. His eyes almost pop out of his head when he sees what's been going on. In just four days, the price of the stock has jumped from about four dollars per share to just over seven dollars! If he's going to catch this one, he has to act quickly.

Johnson goes into his online trading account, where he has roughly $15,000—almost all of his discretionary income. Within five minutes, he owns 200 shares of SPBR. Signing off, he mops his brow and goes to find his wife to tell her the good news. But then he stops himself. He decides to wait a few days. He wants to see the stock price climb a bit first. He smiles to himself as he anticipates telling her about his amazing purchase.

Not only does the stock price climb over the next couple of days—it soars. Soon, Johnson has doubled his investment. He fills his wife in, and she's jubilant. At last they're getting a lucky break. She starts dreaming of exotic vacations and a very comfortable retirement.

Johnson has a hunch that the price climb is just beginning. It's now November, and he's looking forward to a great Christmas. In the space of three days, the daily trading volume of the Spectrum shares rises from 25,000 to 33,000. After that, the share price bounces around a little, dipping slightly over the next week, but nothing severe. Johnson knows from previous experience that price shifts occur as investors take their profits. He's tempted to sell off a little of his own position, but instead he waits it out. In fact, he thinks that if he sees any real forward movement in the stock price, he'll buy some more.

Then he receives another e-mail from Spectrum. This time it's signed by the CEO, a Michael J. Burns. Burns is predicting that Spectrum's stock price will peak at about $15. This reassures Johnson, and he establishes $15 as his price target. The next time he sees the stock price approach this figure, he'll sell.

Two weeks before Christmas, Johnson awakes from a fitful night's sleep and boots up his computer. His heart sinks as he pulls up the stock price. His gold mine, his ticket to riches, has plummeted to $.14 per share. His savings have vanished, and all his big dreams evaporate in a second. He clicks desperately through various Web pages in an attempt to find out what has gone so terribly wrong with Spectrum Brands Corporation and its wondrous technology. Over the next few days, it becomes clear to him that he's been scammed.

*   *   *

Although this scenario is fictitious, it contains factual information concerning the Spectrum Brands Corporation scam. The real story of this fraud is a fascinating one.

On September 21, 2001, just ten days after the terrorist attacks on the World Trade Center and the Pentagon, a dormant, publicly traded shell company called Spectrum Brands (SPBR), headquartered in Boca Raton, Florida, filed the controversial form called S-8 with the SEC. This filing effectively registered a million shares of the shell's common stock to be issued, "from time to time, to certain officers, directors, employees, and qualified consultants." Shortly thereafter, in October, the principals of the shell company began negotiating to sell the entity to a group later described in an SEC litigation release as "the Galasso crew." This crew was headed by convicted racketeer Saverio (Sammy) Galasso III, who was allegedly associated with the Colombo family of the Cosa Nostra. Galasso's key henchmen were David Hutter (aka David Green), Charlie Dilluvio, and Michael J. Burns.

During the last week of October, Galasso and Dilluvio, along with their attorney, Charles J. Cassandro, wrapped up negotiations for the purchase of the shell and transferred $275,000 to the former principals of the company in exchange for a controlling position. Burns signed the appropriate papers and became SPBR's sole officer, director, and employee. About three days later, in accordance with the S-8 filing, the group began issuing themselves common stock. Apparently, 400,000 shares went to the company's original principals, and the remaining 600,000 were issued to Dilluvio and Cassandro. Being an officer of the company, Burns received restricted stock—one million shares.

Over the following week, the crew continued to issue themselves stock. Three million unrestricted shares went to Dilluvio, Cassandro, and other members of the crew; two million unrestricted shares were paid to the prior principals of the shell company; and five million restricted shares were paid to the figurehead Burns as a five-for-one stock dividend (five million to the original one million issued earlier).

While Galasso and Dilluvio were sealing the deal on the shell company, Galasso crew member David Hutter, using the alias David Green, called on a company named Spectronics, located in Westbury, New York. Spectronics owned a product

called the DeGERMinator, a handheld device that could purportedly wipe out bacteria, viruses, and microorganisms. The
product's distributor was one Joseph Schulman of Lakewood,
New Jersey, and he'd been selling the DeGERMinator through
his website. Hutter entered into talks with Schulman with the
aim of buying for Spectrum the exclusive distribution rights for
the DeGERMinator. Spectrum's interest had been piqued by
speculation that the device could destroy anthrax bacteria.

Hutter explained to Schulman that Spectrum wanted
three things out of the deal: the distribution rights for the
DeGERMinator; Schulman's consent to serve as SPBR's CEO;
and the right to purchase Shulman's website and toll-free
number. Schulman signed a contract to this effect, but Spectrum never countersigned it. Instead, in a November 1 press
release, the crew announced that Michael Burns would be the
chairman and CEO of Spectrum Brands. In that press release,
there was no mention of any member of the Galasso crew. It was
abundantly clear to Shulman that he had no deal. He'd been
shut out.

Once again, Hutter approached Spectronics. This time, he
offered to buy 1,000 DeGERMinators directly from the company. Spectrum paid Spectronics $35,000 for the devices, but
by the end of November the crew had failed to pick up the shipment of the product they were supposedly distributing.

On November 5, Spectrum posted this claim on its website:
the DeGERMinator is capable of "wiping out surface germs in
less than five seconds, including anthrax." The company did
not, however, make one crucial distinction. The anthrax bacteria and the anthrax spore are two different things. The anthrax
spore invades the human or animal host, and there it develops

into a deadly bacteria, which brings on the anthrax disease. The claim that the DeGERMinator wipes out anthrax is therefore false. Any product capable of wiping out anthrax would have to kill both the spores and the bacteria. In other words, the DeGERMinator was not the enormous boon to humanity it seemed to be. For this reason, the SEC, in its December litigation release, deemed Spectrum's website claim materially inaccurate and misleading. It was nothing more than a ploy to push SPBR's stock price.

Another such ploy was an interview with Jon Cooper of Spectronics (the one that had so impressed the fictitious Wayne Johnson). The interview aired at the beginning of November on Long Island's Channel 12, and in it Cooper maintained that the DeGERMinator could very well be effective in destroying anthrax spores. Several days later, however, Cooper contacted Charles Cassandro, the Galasso crew's lawyer, to recant that claim. He told Cassandro that he did not believe that the device could actually destroy the spores. Still, SPBR maintained its website link to the Cooper interview for another week.

These activities, in conjunction with various press releases and a massive spam e-mail campaign, began to work their insidious magic on Spectrum's stock price. But the pump's big push was the volume manipulation orchestrated by Charlie Dilluvio.

Dilluvio, the principal of his own financial firm, Windsor Capital LLC, manipulated the volume of the stock by buying and selling it through his own account at Windsor. This trading activity falsely represented an active market for SPBR stock, luring unsuspecting investors. On November 2, SPBR's total market volume was 25,440 shares, with 13,800 shares (54 percent of the total daily market volume) traded in Dilluvio's account. By November 6, the total market volume had risen to 71,195 shares, with only 8,000 shares (11 percent of the total daily market volume) traded in Dilluvio's account. This drove Spectrum's price from an already inflated seven dollars per share on November 2 to $14 per share on November 5. All of this was based on the self-generated Spectrum news and the volume manipulation. SPBR still had no assets or revenue.

Through the first week of November, various members of the Galasso crew began selling off their shares, and this activity may have been what finally nudged SPBR onto law-enforcement's radar screens. The stock dump, coupled with a Bloomberg news service article questioning the company's claims concerning the DeGERMinator, sent SPBR's price into a downward spiral. On December 10, it hit $1.91. The next day, Galasso, Dilluvio, Hutter, and Burns were arrested by authorities acting as agents of the U.S. Attorney's Office on charges of federal securities fraud. Galasso and Hutter, who were out on bail awaiting sentencing for previous crimes, were sent immediately to jail to await a hearing on the new charges.

It is likely that the SEC will order Galasso and his crew to pay restitution to their victims, but those unfortunate and trusting investors may wait a long time to get any of their money back. Much depends on how long the perpetrators are in prison and how well they do financially after they get out. Money made in these scams is usually spent as quickly as it appears; either that, or it's transferred to offshore accounts during the course of the crime.

*　*　*

Online investing can be very dangerous. People who seek out their own opportunities on the Internet are more likely to look at investments they would otherwise have scoffed at, simply because they happen upon these investments themselves. The relaxed investor, surfing the Web, dabbling in stock research during his or her spare time, is open to suggestion. The investor who is interrupted while engaged in some leisure activity by a hectoring phone call from a slick cold-calling broker will instinctively resist the product being pushed.

It is important to remember that anyone can buy a domain name and post anything at all on the site. Fraudsters can make something look thoroughly legitimate and very enticing, or they can set up links to misleading interviews, broadcasts, or press releases. The Internet is a vast maze of traps and hiding places. The following real-life case provides a vivid demonstration of what can befall the investor who fails to scrutinize an offered deal.

On July 19, 1999, a press release was issued by a company called Uniprime Capital Acceptance (UPCA). Uniprime had some thrilling news to announce to the world: it had found a cure for AIDS. That cure took the form of a product called Plasma Plus. The Internet buzzed with it. AIDS sufferers and their loved ones rejoiced, and investors speculated that buying into UPCA would be like buying into Microsoft or Yahoo! before they became household names. Uniprime's share price shot from about one dollar to over seven dollars, with an estimated five million shares trading in one day.

And why not? Plasma Plus was reversing the effects of HIV in 100 percent of patients tested, and even at seven bucks a share it was a steal! Furthermore, the tests on it had been performed by "honorary" immunologist Alfred Flores. These tests, conducted mainly in 1990 at the University of Madrid, proved that Plasma Plus and Flores's company, New Technologies and Concepts (the 70 percent owner of which was Uniprime), had made the breakthrough of the century. There was no doubt that UPCA investors were poised to strike it rich.

Too good to be true? Absolutely. It was all a hoax, and legions of investors—hopeful, unsuspecting, and, let's face it, just plain greedy—lost hundreds of thousands of their hard-earned dollars. Flores was an audacious fraudster. Neither the University of Madrid nor the University of Colorado, the two institutions Flores claimed had awarded him honorary degrees, had ever heard of him. Not to mention the fact that during the time he was supposed to have been conducting his studies at the University of Colorado, Flores was actually serving the last stretch of a nine-year prison term. He'd been convicted of conspiring to commit murder for financial gain.

And that's not all. None of the doctors cited in UPCA press releases, doctors who had purportedly offered testimonials to the effectiveness of Plasma Plus and the authenticity of the tests, had ever heard of Flores either. Nor had the patients whose names were attached to testimonials to the efficacy of the product. It came down to this: Uniprime existed on paper; Plasma Plus, the research results, and the information in the press releases were fabricated.

The SEC acted quickly. On July 22, 1999, the commission halted trading in UPCA stock. Remarkably, however, UPCA and Flores continued to sell shares of the company in what they termed a "private placement," commandeering an estimated $500,000 in investor money. The SEC action expired two weeks later, on August 4, and UPCA stock was once again trading over the counter. In the two weeks following the expiration of the SEC injunction, an estimated 800,000 shares were traded.

Then, on August 13, 1999, Flores was arrested in Manhattan. The SEC had filed an emergency action against Uniprime and Flores, and through a coordinated effort with the United States Attorney's Office, the commission had finally nailed the Plasma Plus fraudsters. The action enjoined them from continuing the fraud and it had a provision seeking to bar Flores from ever acting as a corporate director again. The fraudsters were temporarily defanged, and their assets were frozen. Flores was imprisoned.

*   *   *

Internet regulation is a whole new frontier. For this reason, the technology attracts unsavory people who see it as a means to exploit others from behind the Net's shield of anonymity. Two factors—this shield and the Net's millions of users worldwide—make it an ideal medium for investment scamming. Investment fraud conducted via the Internet benefits from vastly increased scale and drastically reduced overhead. Investors exploring online opportunities must utilize all of the safety precautions that apply to other forms of investing. To ignore those precautions, or to overlook them in the heat of the moment, is to invite disaster.

But sometimes it doesn't matter how careful you are or how much research you do. You get robbed anyway. Robert C. Ingardia, a 25-year-old New York stockbroker, managed to fleece a number of relatively savvy investors.

The SEC alleges that between June and August of 2001, Ingardia, working in concert with several unnamed co-conspirators, manipulated the markets for the stocks of two companies: Converge Global (Utah-based and headquartered in Santa Monica, California) and Equity Technologies and Resources (Delaware-based and headquartered in Lexington, Kentucky). The stocks of both these companies were penny stocks; that is, they traded for less than five dollars per share and were not listed on any of the national or regional exchanges.

Ingardia worked for the boutique brokerage Joseph Stevens. Before that, he'd learned the ropes at six other firms, and while doing so he'd been privy to a tremendous amount of confidential client information—social security numbers, dates of birth, addresses, bank account locations, other brokerage account locations. Using that privileged information, Ingardia stole the identities of Joseph Stevens clients and clients of the other firms he'd worked for. He used the stolen identities to transact business within his victims' primary brokerage accounts—accounts at firms like Charles Schwab, Brown, and Fidelity. First, Ingardia would liquidate the stock positions in a given account. Then, using the proceeds from the liquidation, he would purchase shares of Converge Global and/or Equity Technologies and Resources (ETCR).

Using identity theft to manipulate the markets was a new take on the old pump and dump. This time, however, unsuspecting investors were not being cajoled into buying worthless stocks; they were buying them unintentionally. According to the SEC, Ingardia and his cohorts executed approximately $1.1 million in unauthorized trades in the accounts of their victims, including the liquidation of nearly $800,000 worth of stock positions.

The SEC stated, "Transactions effected by Ingardia accounted for a large percentage of all shares traded of Converge and ETCR on those days."

The illicit proceeds were used to buy an estimated one million shares of Converge and an estimated two million shares of ETCR. On many occasions, the fraudsters bought the securities in smaller blocks and in successive trades at graduating prices in the textbook pump-and-dump fashion. This allowed Ingardia's co-conspirators to dump their positions at the highest possible prices. On September 9, 2001, within three days of the SEC's action, Ingardia was arrested under the authority of the U.S. Attorney's Office for the Southern District of New York and charged with securities fraud.

To establish and conduct business in any financial account, one must provide the institution that maintains the account with certain personal information. Ingardia began with the basic proof of identity—social security numbers and dates of birth—but in order to move forward with the scam, he had to have information on account locations and content. He took this key information from standard account forms, and from there he launched into his fraud operation. Only someone with access to privileged information could have enacted this scheme.

* * *

Some people believe that when it comes to business practices, if it's legal, then it's ethical. But such a definition is too narrow. Certain practices may be legal and exploitative at the same time. It is ethically questionable to mislead clients or otherwise take advantage of their lack of knowledge and sophistication. One dubious practice favored by unethical investment-world types involves "toxic" convertibles, or "death spiral" financing.

After the dot-com bubble burst in 2000, many companies, especially growth-oriented Internet businesses, found themselves in dire financial straits. Companies that had enjoyed astoundingly successful IPOs were suddenly unable to raise funds through secondary offerings in the new environment of investor panic and despair. Nowadays, with the economy lumbering along and the markets in limbo, IPOs and secondary offerings seem like a happy memory—they belong to a distant era, before investor disillusionment. Many companies, especially at the microcap level, are fighting to survive, and for this reason they are easy prey for unethical capital investors. Here's how toxic convertibles work.

The fraudster peruses the microcap markets, such as the OTC Bulletin Board or the Pink Sheets, and selects a small, struggling company. He approaches the company's management, offering to inject capital into the enterprise in the form of a loan secured by "convertible" securities—preferred stocks, bonds, or debentures that can be swapped for common shares of the company. The problem lies in what is called the "reset provision." This provision gives the holders of the convertibles the right to execute the swap if the share price of the borrowing company's stock falls below a certain market price. The management of some struggling companies sincerely believes that such a loan will save their enterprise, never suspecting that the financier who has offered them the loan is anticipating a drop in the company's stock price. They are in the minority.

Most principals of these struggling companies are in collusion with the fraudulent financier. They are counting on the relatively small cash injection—usually a few million dollars—to buy them time to get their bail-out plans in order and draw more salary money out of the failing company. The financier wants the share price to drop so he can convert his securities into common shares and dump them on the market for a quick profit. And, of course, he has no qualms about manipulating that price drop. He does this by short selling. Although collusive short selling is illegal, those involved in toxic-convertible rings set up their operations through offshore entities, making their activities extremely difficult for regulators to monitor.

Because the trading volume in the stock of the targeted company is light to begin with and the float is small, the share price falls quickly and dramatically in response to the downward pressure put on the stock by the short-selling group. Once the share price falls below the price indicated in the reset provision, the fraudulent financier converts and cashes out. Anyone still holding the stock is left holding the bag.

While organized short selling is illegal, issuing toxic convertibles is not. This is where the question of ethics comes into play. Company principals who are pessimistic about the fate of their enterprises can resort to issuing toxics and still hold to the letter of the law, but in squeezing the last drops of blood from their dying companies, they are betraying their shareholders. There is very little protection available to these shareholders, because most death-spiral financing activity occurs in the realm of penny stocks and microcaps, and the exchanges these stocks list on have lax registration and filing rules. Most investors will not even know that toxics have been issued until it is too late.

* * *

Although many of the scams described in this book utilize securities that are practically worthless, these securities do in fact exist. However, there are scams that involve securities that are pure fiction. One type of nonexistent security that has recently received a lot of press is the "prime bank security." (It may also be called a "revolving credit guarantee," a "high-yield investment program," or a "standby letter of credit.")

The scam that these securities are used for usually unfolds like this. The fraudster contacts an investor and solicits that investor to purchase debt securities—that is, obligations by the issuer (the fraudster) to pay the purchaser (the investor) back. The bond is the simplest form of debt security. The issuer makes interest payments periodically and repays the full amount of the loan at the end of the term of the securities. Payments are to be made through a bank in a foreign country. One hundred of the world's leading banks, the issuer assures the purchaser, are securing the offering. These banks are called prime banks, hence the term "prime bank security." Confidently, the investor buys some of these rock-solid securities.

When the first payment is due, the issuer will fail to make it, giving some legitimate-sounding excuse, like, "Today is a national bank holiday," or, "There's been a glitch in the wire transfer, but it will be cleared up soon." Of course, the investor now has a big problem that will never be cleared up.

The only way to avoid a scam like this is to employ common sense. The investor must have the patience to research all investment opportunities thoroughly, and he or she should be wary of anyone promising unusually high rates of return. Some prime bank–securities fraudsters have boasted returns of over 600 percent! Such inflated promises should be a red flag to any investor. The average stock market return over the past 50 years is about 12 percent, and this figure should be used as a guide to determine whether an investment instrument is being overhyped.

* * *

Finally, there are two more kinds of fraud that the investor should be aware of. First, there is affinity fraud, which plays upon the investor's sense of community. Easily defined groups—religious, racial, professional, even gender groups—are often targeted by fraudsters who practice this particular form of deceit. And because these groups are so broad, anyone can be the target of an affinity scam. Simply put, the affinity fraudster wins an investor's trust by claiming unity with that person through their shared affiliation with a given group.

Then there is "churning"—the act of trading a client's account excessively and unnecessarily without regard for fiduciary responsibility. Churning is the name of the game on the retail side of the securities business. The fraudster finds out as much as possible about an investor's financial situation and uses that information to conduct as much business as possible. It's all about gross sales. For this reason, churning can only happen in brokerages that pay their dealers a commission. In firms where churning goes on, daily sales meetings are held and commissions are announced. Those with the highest sales figures gain status within the brokerage. They are dubbed "producers," and rookies look up to them with admiration. Two battle cries have often been heard on the boiler-room floor: "Pay yourself!" and "Churn and burn!"

Commission-based brokering ("Pay yourself!") is rapidly becoming a thing of the past—most brokers and financial advisers are moving to the fee-based method of payment. But during the bull market of the 1990s, commissions were the norm, and the more trades a broker made in an investor's account, the more cash would wind up in his or her pocket.

There's a rule of thumb in the industry—"the 2-6-8 rule"—that all investors should follow: if the total equity in an investor's account turns over twice in a year, that's normal; if it turns over six times, it's questionable and should be scrutinized; if it turns over eight or more times, it's being churned.

* * *

The prospect of getting entangled in scams like these is very intimidating to many investors, particularly those who are new to the world of investing. But investors should bear in mind a figure mentioned earlier in this book: these crimes are perpetrated by less than one percent of all securities-industry professionals. Furthermore, the vast majority of companies traded on the NYSE and the NASDAQ exchanges are legitimate. So how do we, as investors, protect ourselves against fraud? We painstakingly scrutinize offerings on the OTC Bulletin Board and the Pink Sheets markets, and we carefully research all investment opportunities. If we take these precautions consistently, then our chances of making legitimate investment decisions are strong.

One last pitfall we must avoid is allowing our expectations to get out of control. The bull market of the 1990s created unrealistic expectations in the minds of investors, and many came to expect early retirements and quick riches. It was too good to last, and it didn't. We must now adjust our perspective and view investing as a lifetime project, slowly accruing.

7

A Stranger in the Land
of Opportunity

EXPOSÉ

The year 1987 was the most transitional that 35-year-old Kang Hsu had ever experienced. The bottom fell out of the global economy, taking with it the Asian markets, and Hsu, a commodities broker living in Malaysia, found himself out of a job. He and his wife had just had their first child. After talking it over with an uncle of his, the director of a Malaysian company, Hsu made a difficult decision: he and his small family would leave their homeland and go to the United States. American markets were depressed as well, but Hsu believed that the U.S. could offer him more opportunities than he could hope to have in Asia.

Some cousins living in San Francisco were generous enough to help Hsu and his family get started. Hsu found a job with what his relatives called an ABC (American-born Chinese) produce business, hauling vegetables off trucks and delivering them to a Chinatown farmer's market. Hsu joked to his wife that before this, the heaviest thing he'd ever lifted was a bowl of rice and a pair of chopsticks. Still, their lack of funds was no laughing matter. Hsu badly wanted to earn more money, and quickly.

Every day, he scoured the *San Francisco Chronicle* in search of a higher-paying job. When he spied a small ad in the classifieds for trainee securities brokers, he decided to apply. With his background in commodities, he was confident that he could learn the business quickly.

The company that had placed the ad was a mid-sized boutique brokerage called Franklin Jones, headquartered in New York. The firm's San Francisco branch was its most competitive; its top brokers pulled in between $50,000 and $100,000 a month—serious high rollers. The firm was a mint. It was always hiring new brokers, and those who couldn't hack it were chewed up and spit out in record time. Franklin Jones brokers were allowed to cold call from the office phones, but they weren't paid until they passed the Series 7 licensing exam. Jon Andersen, the branch manager, did the hiring, and he wasn't picky. Any broker who failed the exam was welcome to stick around and give it one more shot. In the meantime, Andersen had unpaid labor to collect hot leads for the office closers.

So, when Hsu presented himself to Andersen and asked in broken English for a chance to prove himself, the manager just smiled and said, "Sure, Mr. Hsu. You can start whenever you want." Hsu wasted no time. Finding an empty desk and a phone, he grabbed the White Pages and got to work. Hsu understood Asian business culture well enough to start compiling a list of leads in the Asian community. He also spoke fluent Mandarin, and that won him access to investors a broker without the language could never have even approached.

Although he studied hard for a month, Hsu failed the exam.
By the time he tried again, however—a month later—his English
had improved somewhat, and he squeaked through. Still, there
were other hurdles he'd have to leap before he could make
money. For one thing, he had to win the respect of his Franklin
Jones superiors, and they were a tough bunch for anyone to
impress.

The firm organized its brokers into quads—groups of four.
Each quad had a leader whose job it was to mentor the other
three quad members. Quad selection worked much the way
schoolyard ball-team selections do. The top guy says, "I'll take
you, and you, and you . . ." until only the undesirables are left
standing awkwardly by the fence. None of Franklin Jones's quad
leaders would choose Hsu—it just didn't seem like he was going
to make it, so why bother with him? But Hsu was by nature confident and resilient, so he pushed on alone, without a mentor.
After all, he reasoned, he had commodities brokering experience (which no one at Franklin Jones knew about), and it gave
him an edge.

He sure had something. By his second month, he was attracting attention. By his third month, he was the top-producing
rookie of all 30 Franklin Jones branch offices. Hsu had found
his calling. In no time, he'd gone from zero to hero. Month four
saw Hsu appointed quad leader, and his quad quickly became
one of the top-producing teams in the firm. His admiring fellow
brokers bestowed upon him a nickname: Kokster, a variation on
part of his full name.

Franklin Jones focused primarily on IPOs of small startups,
usually debuting at $.25 or lower. Although today the situation
is different, back then, in the late 1980s, it was legal for broker-

ages to be self-clearing—that is, they could approve their own trades and clear them through their own routes. At that time, as well, stocks were quoted in fractions. For instance, a penny stock could be worth 1/8, and the spread could have a bid of 1/4 by the ask of 1/2, leaving a difference of 1/4. Since Franklin Jones was self-clearing, the brokerage could retain the excess 1/4 per share and distribute it among deserving (or not so deserving) parties. It's easy to see how these fractions could add up in block transactions of several hundred thousand shares.

At Franklin Jones, the floor, where 40-plus brokers would gather each day to sling IPOs and other stock, was jumping. It was called the bullpen, and Kokster thrived there, feeding off the excitement and energy. He and his compatriots were making money hand over fist. Hsu became good friends with a broker named Buddy Seals. Seals was only 20 years old, and, as the son of a big-shot San Jose attorney, he had a rich-kid ego, but he was good on the phone. And that skill caused his ego to swell even more: on one occasion, he pulled in a commission of almost $30,000. Seals was good—damn good.

Andersen was so pleased with Seals's results that he rewarded him by bringing a stripper in to the office to perform for him one afternoon. The striptease started right there on the floor, but as things heated up, Andersen slipped the girl a couple of C-notes, and her act became a private show for Seals in a back office. Nobody knew for sure if she did anything more than strip—Seals wouldn't say—but the two of them were in there with the door closed for more than an hour.

In this environment, the less successful brokers felt constant frustration. One of the frustrated underachievers was a gargantuan guy named Lars Sanders. Sanders had been a linebacker

in high school, and he'd played for San Francisco State until a
knee injury scuttled his chances for a pro career. He never got
over the blow that fate had dealt him, and he talked incessantly
to his co-workers about his glory days on the gridiron.

While Sanders may have been a decent ballplayer, he was a
dud of a salesman. One of the guys in his quad, an accomplished salesman named Dillon Marshall who happened to be
flamboyantly gay, never let him forget it. Marshall derived great
satisfaction from taunting Sanders: he flaunted his own suc-
cesses; he mocked Sanders's big, dumb athlete image; and he
implied that Sanders could make more money "playing ball"
with him. All the other brokers on the floor would laugh at this,
and Sanders would struggle to keep his temper under control.

Then one afternoon he lost it. It started out as a shoving
match, and it ended with Sanders shouting, "Fuck you, you
Tennessee fairy!" and hurling Marshall against a wall with a
barroom-style haymaker. Sanders's outburst cost the firm dearly.
Franklin Jones backed Sanders, claiming that his tormentor had
used overly aggressive hazing tactics, so Marshall sued his em-
ployer for discrimination. The suit was settled out of court in
Marshall's favor for an undisclosed sum.

Through distracting incidents like these, Kokster kept his
head down and concentrated on his work—but he also maintained a sense of humor. Soon, he was able to hire his own assistants, and in the job interview he conducted with one of them,
the Kokster humor was clearly in evidence. The interviewee
told him that he had a BS from a state university. Hsu inquired
whether this stood for "bullshit." Offended, the interviewee
asked Hsu if he had a degree himself, like an MBA. "Yeah, I
have an MBA," replied Kokster—"married but available!" They
laughed, and Kokster hired the kid on the spot.

This was Kokster's personality. He could be lighthearted and fun-loving, but he also took his responsibilities very seriously. He was determined not to lose his clients' money. But, although he didn't yet know it, Franklin Jones was undermining his good intentions. Andersen and his assistant branch manager, Phil Lilly, were fiddling with the books.

Lilly was a notorious yes-man, and Kokster couldn't stand him. He would sometimes vent his irritation by messing with Lilly's head and taking a good-natured swipe at his boss. For instance, he'd wait until he had an audience and then say to Andersen and Lilly, "Wise men think alike." Lilly and Andersen would take this as flattery and emphatically agree. Then, after a well-timed comic pause, Kokster would add, "but fools seldom differ."

The other brokers would get a good laugh out of this—it was always fun to see management come in for a little ridicule. Andersen took it well; Lilly did not. He tried everything he could think of to get Hsu fired, going so far as to allege that Hsu was promising clients profit on IPO transactions. Hsu was deeply insulted by this. Sure, he made fun of Lilly once in awhile, but this was no excuse for casting aspersions on his professional honor, which was of the utmost importance to him. Hsu started to think about taking his bulging client book to another firm. But before he could act, the decision was made for him.

Franklin Jones had involved itself in some dubious IPOs—in particular, one involving an AIDS home-test-kit manufacturer, which had netted Hsu a lot of cash—and in so doing had alerted the SEC and the NASD. These agencies suspected that the brokerage had manipulated the stock price by bouncing its stock inventory between itself and another market maker. They launched an investigation.

The investigators didn't unearth anything incriminating in this regard, but they did discover some bookkeeping discrepancies. The IRS called an audit. This was the beginning of the end for Franklin Jones. The audit revealed that the firm had hired its brokers as independent contractors. As this method of compensation was disallowed, Franklin Jones ended up owing hundreds of thousands of dollars in back taxes on the commissions it had paid to brokers over the previous few years.

Andersen, an American citizen, was also a citizen of the Bahamas, so he was able to wire the funds remaining in the branch's accounts to an island tax shelter. He, of course, followed the money, and no one ever heard from him again. Within six months, the entire company was under IRS indictment for tax evasion. It was Kokster's turn to jump ship, before that ship disappeared beneath the waves. Taking his client book, he went looking for work.

Within a day, he'd landed a job with another brokerage, Bay View Capital. His track record spoke for itself, so this time he was spared the hassle of proving himself. He just set himself up and got right down to business. Kokster had come up in the world. At Bay View, he literally had a bay view. He had his own office overlooking the Bay Bridge. One incentive the firm offered its brokers was a bottle of good wine for every $1,000 in gross sales. By the time he left Bay View, Kokster had built quite a collection.

It became his custom to pop a cork every day at noon. Junior brokers would come to him holding out their cups, begging for a taste of the grape. Hsu would sit back and sip from a crystal glass he'd bought at a downtown boutique, gazing out at the bay and calmly talking his clients into the next big thing. At last, Hsu felt that he'd really made it.

Before coming to America, he'd barely been able to drink an entire bottle of beer, let alone a bottle of wine. But during his time in the investment-world trenches, he'd developed certain habits, like meeting local clients in bars to celebrate deal closings. In the process, he'd gone from being a one-beer wonder to a full-blown alcoholic. One day, Kokster grossed over $4,000, so he was in line to receive four bottles of fine wine. He was eager to collect, but Bay View's management had taken off early for the track, and there was no one around to present him with the wine. This was unacceptable to Kokster—he'd earned that prize fair and square, and he should have it.

He knew that the wine was stored in the office kitchen under lock and key, so, drawing upon skills picked up during his misspent youth, he jimmied the lock and helped himself. And not only did he take his own four bottles, but he also selected one for every broker who was still on the floor that day. Kokster felt like Robin Hood—many of these guys would never make it past their first month, but they deserved a good bottle of wine for their efforts. Of course, when his superiors found out what he'd done, they were furious, and they deducted the cost of the wine from his commissions, but Kokster didn't care. It was a small price to pay for that much fun.

By this time, Kokster was also altering his mind with cocaine, LSD, and marijuana. He was making more money than he had ever thought possible, and he'd moved his family into a nice downtown apartment. His wife liked to keep busy, so she took a job at a small neighborhood bar, but their lifestyle depended on Hsu's earnings. Since ready cash and a growing reliance on drugs and alcohol were seriously altering Kokster's idea of a good time, that lifestyle was not nearly as secure as he and his wife believed.

The broker community in any city is relatively small, and that of San Francisco was no exception. After work, many members of that community would meet at a bar aptly named The Exchange, which happened to be right around the corner from Bay View. On one particular evening, Kokster was there drinking with colleagues from several different firms. One of these colleagues was a broker Kokster had worked with at Franklin Jones. Miguel Presto was a heavyset man with greasy hair and a clammy handshake. After the demise of Franklin Jones, he'd ended up at a firm called Pacific Coast Securities.

Like Kokster, Presto had prospered in the business, and he used his money to indulge his appetite for the extreme, mixing his perversions with his own brand of humor. That night at The Exchange, the drinking group that Kokster and Presto belonged to numbered nine. They decided to move the party into one of the bar's back rooms. The bar's management gave access to these rooms, which had locking doors, to their big-spender customers. Like they'd done so many times before, the revelers shut themselves in and got down to boasting about their antics. Kokster was conversing intently with another broker about moving to yet another firm, and he didn't want the others to hear their conversation, so they headed back to the front room to continue their talk. On his way, Kokster saw a slender blond enter the private room where his companions were drinking. He assumed she was the girlfriend of one of the brokers and thought nothing of it. After about half an hour, Kokster said goodnight to his conversation partner. He went back to the private room and knocked on the locked door, waiting to be admitted. The door opened just a crack, and Presto peered out. He gave Kokster a crooked smile and motioned for him to slip inside.

The blond was sitting on the lap of one of the brokers. Her makeup was smeared and her hair was tousled. She sipped at a drink, swishing the booze around in her mouth like mouthwash. Presto slapped Kokster on the back and asked him if he wanted the disheveled woman to relieve some of his workday tension for him. Kokster was confused, so Presto explained that the woman was a prostitute he had hired to reward some of his junior brokers. Laughing, Kokster declined the gift, saying that she'd been too well used for his taste. He'd rather start fresh if he was going to go there. The hooker scowled at him and said something rude. This prompted an uproar—all of the assembled brokers, Kokster included, thought it was hilarious. The disgruntled hooker began snatching up her things. Presto tossed a wad of bills in her direction, thanked her curtly, and told her to leave "our bar."

"I'm going to call you guys the Magnificent Seven," Kokster said.

"You mean the Magnificent Six," one of the brokers quipped. "Mendoza here didn't get one!"

Mendoza, one of Presto's junior brokers, explained that he was the last in line for the favor since he was the newest member of the crew. He added that he wasn't interested anyway, because whatever the guys had, he didn't want to catch it. "Yeah," Presto snickered, "Mendoza brought his gun to war, but he didn't use it!" Another round of hysterics. They continued drinking late into the night, and Kokster didn't get home until 3:00 a.m. Needless to say, his wife was not happy.

Due to his long working hours and his hard partying, his marriage was already under a lot of strain. After his late return from The Exchange, Kokster's wife wasn't interested in having sex with him for weeks. Of course, Kokster had exacerbated the situation by telling her, in a drunken moment, all about Presto's "present." Then one night Kokster tried to soften his wife's defenses, and she angrily told him to go to a whorehouse instead. He took her up on the suggestion. One of his friends had told him about a Korean massage parlor where customers experienced very happy endings, so that's where he went. When he arrived, he was introduced to a pretty young Korean woman who treated him like an emperor—she even put on his socks and tied his tie for him after their session.

Kokster had a naïve, childlike streak. He returned home and told his wife all about his "massage." After all, she had told him to go in the first place, and he'd only followed her advice. She listened in silence as he extolled the virtues of the Korean whore, and she went to bed in a state of suppressed rage. The next day, everything seemed normal, and the situation remained that way for nearly two weeks. Lying in bed watching television with his wife one night, Kokster was totally unprepared when she suddenly leaned over and punched him in the chest with all her might. She announced that this was his punishment for visiting the whorehouse.

"But you told me to go," Kokster gasped.

"If I told you to eat shit, would you do that?" she replied.

From that moment on, their marriage unraveled at an accelerated pace. Within two months, Kokster's wife had kicked him out of the house and forbidden him from seeing their child. He spent a couple nights in his office, sleeping on the couch and drinking wine. Eventually, he got a place of his own. Convinced that if he could only change his ways, his wife would take him back, he resolved to do just that. It was a childish notion—of course, things weren't nearly that simple. Kokster's wife was not interested in a reconciliation. She wanted her wayward husband out of her life permanently, so she had him served with a restraining order that prohibited him from having contact with her or their child until a divorce hearing could proceed. Kokster was stunned.

A notice of the restraining order had actually been sent to him, but he hadn't opened his mail in quite awhile. Upon learning of this development, he went straight to his wife's house to protest. When she refused to let him in, he stood outside yelling, unaware that she had called the police. He was arrested and thrown in jail.

Kokster spent three days in jail. When he called his manager at Bay View to let him know where he was, he heard gales of laughter in the background—the manager had put him on the speaker phone. Kokster's only support, apparently, was his attorney, who smuggled packs of cigarettes in to his nicotine-addicted client. This booty gave him the power to establish himself as boss of the holding pen, but he was more interested in getting out of jail and back to his life. He'd finally come to understand that he'd have to work long and hard to win his family back—and that it might not be possible.

Once he was out of the can, Kokster's resolve to change his ways crumbled. He wanted to get back on track, but the task suddenly seemed overwhelming. His wife's rage was as strong as ever, and he had no idea how to quell it. Depressed, Kokster fell back on his vices.

During one of his forays into extreme decadence, he was accompanied by Alison, his pretty brunette sales assistant, who was a fan of crack cocaine. Kokster had never smoked crack before, but Alison kept raving about how good it made her feel, so he decided to give it a try. Approaching Alison one day after market closing, he asked her if she wanted to score some crack, and she said she'd love to. In Kokster's car, they made their way to the seamy Tenderloin district. Before too long, they were flagged down by a shady-looking street-corner dealer, his sweatshirt hood pulled down over his eyes. Alison told him what they were looking for, and he climbed into the back seat, saying that they needed to find a more secluded spot to transact their business. Besides, the dealer added, he had a hankering for a smoke himself, and he didn't want the people he worked for to know he did crack. So Kokster drove around for a while until they found a run-down motel, and they checked in.

In the motel room, the dealer produced the crack, a glass pipe, and a butane lighter. Choking a bit, Kokster inhaled the chemical-laden smoke. Then a warm rush overtook him, making his whole body tingle. It felt great. The three continued to smoke until the dealer announced that he was out. By this time, Kokster was sitting on the bed because he could no longer stand. Alison was beside him, and she started to massage his shoulders and kiss his neck. Beckoning the dealer over to the side of the bed, she proceeded to unzip his pants. Within minutes, hazy with crack, they were engaged in a three-way. That afternoon was beyond Kokster's wildest imaginings.

It seemed that the only thing going right for Kokster was that he was becoming more and more financially successful. He continued to pay his wife's rent and give her money for their child; he was also putting a lot of cash into his own bank account. Still, his relations with his clients did not always go smoothly. Some clients decayed on their stock purchases.

There is a lag time between the client's agreement to buy a stock and the brokerage's receipt of the payment for the stock. It generally takes three or four days for a client's payment check to arrive on the broker's desk, and if in the meantime the stock price falls, then the check may fail to arrive at all. The situation of a client failing to honor his or her promise to buy is called a "decay." When it occurs, the broker who has exacted the promise to buy must cover any losses that take place during the lag time. In the investment world, greed isn't confined to stockbrokers. For every unethical broker there's an unethical investor who will track the markets closely and decay on a stock purchase if that is in his or her best interest. Brokers who have suffered thousands of dollars in decay losses have become embittered by this aspect of the business. For a broker of Kokster's talents, the occasional decay loss is manageable, but for lesser talents or rookies it can be ruinous.

Another type of problem Kokster encountered while at Bay View was having a stock recommendation fall apart. On one occasion, Kokster homed in on a Hungarian manufacturing company that looked fantastic on paper. Its earnings were solid, and its stock price was just beginning to move. He began calling his clients heavily, picking up $20,000 here, $30,000 there. But when he was about $200,000 into the stock, it just disappeared from the boards. Now Kokster was facing a very difficult situation. As it transpired, the company's CEO had embezzled a large amount of the company's cash and then vanished, at which point the SEC suspended trading in the stock pending an investigation. With a lot of coaxing, Kokster got all of his clients to pay for their stock. He was fortunate. Everyone who had purchased the stock lost their money—such are the perils of investing—

and the whole mess didn't do much for Kokster's professional reputation as an adviser.

Many brokers dream of one day opening up their own firm or perhaps brokering an investment-banking deal that will set them up for life. Unfortunately, most lack the means or the talent for it. But Kokster believed that he had both. In the course of his career, he had met some very wealthy individuals and some skilled professionals. He began to ponder ways of combining their money and skills to create a lucrative business opportunity.

One of his clients was Doctor Harvey Simpson. Simpson was, quite simply, a genius. His specialty was hydrodynamics, and he was obsessed with the idea of producing one of his inventions: a more energy-efficient ship's hull. The shipping industry, he insisted to Kokster, needed his improved hull. It would prove to be an invaluable contribution, and he wanted Kokster to help him raise the funds he needed to build a proto-type. Simpson knew that Kokster had many wealthy clients who were always looking for new investment opportunities. The markets were hot, and these people were very receptive to the idea of getting into a technology-based company on the ground floor. Kokster was intrigued.

The first step was to incorporate. Kokster had done his research, and he filed the paperwork to create the corporation, which was called Simpson and Associates. Kokster intended to take the company public further down the line. Part of his plan involved a partnership with two brokers he knew from his Franklin Jones days: the incomparable Buddy Seals, and a former Franklin Jones heavy hitter named David Stalworth. Both men had big client lists, which would come in handy for recruiting the initial investors they needed to get the corporation off the ground; those lists would also be a source of leads when they were ready to sell the stock after the IPO. Two more men were brought to the Simpson team through Kokster's efforts—Ukrainian nationals named Igor and Villa. The five men created a holding company they called FSF Financial—an inside joke, because the acronym stood for Fools of San Francisco. Simpson and Associates would be one of the companies under the FSF umbrella.

Simpson needed time to complete his prototype, so while they waited Kokster and his partners explored other opportunities. One such opportunity was a brewery based in the Ukraine. Igor and Villa knew a group of businessmen—which turned out to be a splinter group of the Russian Mafia—who owned a factory where beer could be made for a fraction of what it would cost in the U.S. The deal was that FSF would raise the money to purchase the raw materials, buy them, and ship them to the Ukrainian factory; the finished product would be shipped back to the U.S. and sold under the name Bay Coast Brewery. The brewing company would go public once the sales revenue started flowing in.

The FSF crew was able to gather together 40 investors willing to finance the purchase and shipping of the raw materials. Seals was in charge of handling the money. Before the deal was finalized, the factory owners flew the FSF partners to the Ukraine to tour the brewing facilities and verify their suitability. Kokster, however, stayed behind to finish working out the distribution details. Seals, Stalworth, Igor, and Villa went off happily and were treated to parties with prostitutes and all the usual perks. When they returned home with stories of drinking bouts and debauchery, Kokster was a bit jealous. He was also a bit worried, all of a sudden, about the true intentions of his Eastern European partners. But the deal was still in motion, and he planned to see it through to the end.

The 40 investors began sending in their money, and the game was on. Overnight, it seemed, Seals's lifestyle started to change. His suits were a lot nicer, and he drove a new car. He assured Kokster and his partners that the money to pay for these improvements came from other ventures, but Kokster was suspicious. He contacted the manufacturers of the raw materials for the brewery operation, and they verified that they had received the appropriate orders. This reassured Kokster somewhat—maybe he was just being paranoid. He relaxed and stopped watching Seals so closely. This was a big mistake.

One afternoon, Igor and Villa came into Kokster's office. Igor was in tears. The two explained that the materials had never reached the factory in the Ukraine, and the factory owners had told them that if those materials or $20,000 did not arrive within three days, then Igor's sister, who lived in Odessa, would be killed. That did it. Kokster audited the books himself, only to discover that Seals's extravagant new lifestyle was being funded from the money sent in by the Bay Coast Brewery investors. And the $20,000—the money earmarked for the first raw-materials shipment—was just the tip of the iceberg; they had collected enough money for a series of shipments, and most of that money had already disappeared.

A furious Kokster realized that he was in an impossible situation. While he and the others were general partners in the company, and were thus liable for investor contributions, Seals had never signed on as a partner himself. There was still just enough money in the account to pay off the Russian mobsters and save Igor's sister, so Kokster made the painful decision to wire them their $20,000.

Buddy Seals got wind of the audit and vanished underground. Shortly after this, Kokster was obliged to meet with the FBI—the bureau had been alerted by worried Bay Coast Brewery investors. Kokster told the feds the whole story, including how he'd transferred funds from the investment account to the mobsters in the Ukraine. But it was Seals the feds were primarily interested in, and they wanted Kokster and Stalworth to help flush him out—they were convinced that the partners knew where Seals was holed up. They didn't, in fact; the intrepid con artist had left them in the dark. The feds insisted that Kokster and Stalworth set up an investors' meeting and get Seals to attend. They wanted Kokster to wear a wire to the meeting in an attempt to entrap Seals. Kokster refused, maintaining that all they had to do to gather the evidence they needed to convict Seals and prove the FSF partners' innocence was to study the paper trail left by Seals. But instead the feds persuaded Stalworth to wear the wire.

David Stalworth wasn't about to take any responsibility for the fiasco, and in his desperation to get himself off the hook, he tried to place the blame on Kokster. The investors' meeting was set for Wednesday at 1 p.m. Without informing Kokster, Stalworth called all 40 investors and changed the time to 11 a.m. Fortunately for Kokster, some of those investors were his loyal friends, so they clued him in. He showed up for the meeting with his attorney, much to the dismay of Stalworth, who had wanted to pull the rug out from under Kokster without any interference.

Then the finger pointing began in earnest. Stalworth told the assembled investors that Kokster was responsible for the fraud because he had decided to put Seals in charge of the money in the first place. Kokster countered that it had been a joint decision. He also added that Stalworth had enjoyed the mobsters' hospitality—that is, the booze and the prostitutes—when he should have been focusing on the brewery inspection. Seals, of course, didn't show up for the meeting.

Since Stalworth and Kokster were liable for the actions of FSF, they owed a debt of gratitude to the FBI in the end. If the feds hadn't been so diligent in their investigation of the FSF fraud, the partners would have faced financial ruin. As it turned out, the bureau apprehended Buddy Seals within a month and tried him for embezzlement and fraud. He was convicted, sentenced to two years in prison, and ordered to pay back the investors in monthly installments upon his release. Kokster and Stalworth got off with only minor disciplinary actions on their records.

Despite this upset, Kokster was still determined to strike out on his own, so he turned his attention to Simpson and the hull design. The prototype was almost ready. Kokster raised the capital necessary to construct the hull on a Vietnam War–era PBR (Proud, Brave, and Reliable) riverboat. He and Simpson arranged to test it with representatives of the U.S. Department of Energy on hand, because they hoped to get a grant from that agency to develop the project further.

The test was scheduled for a sunny July afternoon. Kokster and Simpson stood on the dock with two DOE reps and admired the prototype riverboat. Simpson and one of the officials boarded the vessel, fired up the engines, and made a very impressive run. The new energy-efficient hull was deemed a success by the DOE, and a couple days later Kokster and Simpson received notification that a grant to build an all-new version of the vessel had been awarded to Simpson and Associates, of which Kokster was the CEO. The future was starting to look rosier for Kokster.

He was filled with inspiration, and he fervently applied himself to the project. Grant money was spent, a modernized prototype was fabricated, and everyone involved—including the initial investors—was starting to feel as though this thing could be really big. Kokster's Malaysian uncle, the one who had helped him decide to seek his fortune in the United States, was one of the investors in the endeavor. He informed his nephew that a giant boat show would be taking place in Malaysia in a few months' time, and it would present them with the perfect opportunity to unveil the boat to the Asian business community.

Kokster and Simpson made the arrangements to transport the vessel to Malaysia. The boat show was an extremely popular event—many of Asia's wealthiest businessmen attended, shopping for a new toy or a hot new Western technology that they could distribute to the Asian market. The energy-efficient hull caused a mild sensation, attracting the attention of several top-level executives and a Malaysian prince. Kokster and Simpson were on hand to drink it all in.

Kokster was anxious not to let anything interfere with their good fortune. There was still a lot of work to be done, and he was on it. He wanted to be sure that if they got a bite as a result of the boat show, they had licensing agreements at the ready and were prepared to enter into negotiations. While Kokster went home to work, Simpson stayed behind to present the prototype to interested parties. When several weeks had passed with no word from his partner, Kokster contacted his uncle. He hadn't seen or heard from Simpson either. Then one day Simpson walked into Kokster's office, visibly nervous.

He had been treated like a celebrity in Malaysia—relentlessly wined and dined. Then an Asian businessman had given him $30,000 for certain rights to the invention. But what Simpson had failed to understand was that he'd actually sold the prototype outright to the businessman, his gracious host at many dinners. As soon as the full import of what he'd done had dawned on him, he'd tried to get the contract annulled, but Asian business culture was incomprehensible to him, and he was thwarted at every turn. The Department of Energy–sponsored vessel was unrecoverable.

Kokster got on the phone and frantically tried to undo the damage his partner had done, but it was too late. There was no way that boat was leaving Malaysia. Neither Kokster nor Simpson could face informing the Department of Energy of this turn of events, so their only option was to bury the project. The unpleasant task of apprising the investors fell to Kokster. He reluctantly told them about the mishandling of the project and let them know that Simpson and Associates would be dissolved.

Once again, doing business in a foreign country had ended disastrously for Kokster. By now his divorce was well under way, and his dream of making it as an independent businessman was destroyed. So Kokster decided to go back to what he did best—slinging stock.

8

The Regulators

As we've seen, criminals and unethical businesspeople exploit the complexity of the markets to take money from investors rather than make money for them. They are undeterred by the fact that their manipulations directly affect the nation's economic health and the quality of life enjoyed by its citizens.

Companies that employ millions of Americans are listed on the U.S. stock exchanges, and when market trends affect the stock prices of these companies, their employees often feel the repercussions—layoffs and pension-plan losses can wreak havoc with people's lives. Furthermore, millions of Americans are private investors, pinning their hopes and dreams—their children's education, their plans for a comfortable retirement—on the securities markets. So when fraudsters create an environment of distrust in these markets, they do untold damage. White collar crime is egregious—it's a myth that it harms no one. It is a form of greed that erodes the national well-being.

Certain organizations, both federal and private, have been established over the years to combat this type of criminal activity. These organizations are mandated to create, maintain, and protect an environment of ethical practice within the securities markets.

The most renowned of these regulating organizations is the federally established Securities and Exchange Commission. The SEC's primary responsibilities are to protect investors and to uphold the integrity of the various securities markets. To this end, the commission has established rules of conduct that deal specifically with the disclosure of pertinent information and with the protection of investors. The SEC has jurisdiction over stock exchanges, broker-dealers, mutual funds, public-utility holding companies, and investment advisers, and it is empowered to enforce securities laws with regard to these entities and their respective relationships with investors.

After the Wall Street crash of 1929, the problems caused by the lack of regulation in the securities industry became apparent. President Franklin Delano Roosevelt decided that his government must intervene in order to stabilize the economy and lay the foundation for future prosperity. So, on May 26, 1933, Congress approved the Securities Act of 1933, also called the Truth in Securities Act. The act decrees that companies must register their securities before offering them publicly. Companies are also obligated to disclose all positive and negative aspects of their enterprise, and this information should be presented in the form of a prospectus to anyone who is considering a purchase of its offering.

The SEC was created by Congress through the Securities Act of 1934 to enforce the 1933 act. One of its functions was to help stabilize market conditions; but the commission was primarily established to protect investors and restore public faith in the integrity of the securities markets. Roosevelt appointed Joseph P. Kennedy (patriarch of the Kennedy clan) as the commission's first chairman (despite rumors that he'd been involved in bootlegging during Prohibition, which ended in 1933).

The commission is headed up by five commissioners who are appointed by the president of the United States. Each commissioner serves a five-year term. Each term is staggered so that every year on June 5, one commissioner's term elapses. To avoid partisan agendas, no more than three commissioners can be members of the same political party. The highest-ranking commissioner is the chairman.

All meetings of the SEC are open to the public and the news media, except meetings in which a decision about whether to launch an investigation must be made—these sessions are confidential. Most meetings of the commission concern the interpretation and/or the amendment of federal securities legislation; the evaluation of market conditions and the proposition of new rules to meet any changing conditions; and the enforcement of SEC rules and federal securities law.

The SEC is comprised of four divisions: the Division of Corporation Finance, the Division of Market Regulation, the Division of Investment Management, and the Division of Enforcement. The primary function of the Division of Corporation Finance is to review the filings submitted by public companies in compliance with the disclosure laws—such things as annual and quarterly reports, proxy documents sent to shareholders, documents regarding tender offers, and registrations for new securities issues.

This division also reviews documents concerning filings for mergers and acquisitions. Again, the purpose of this is to provide investors with all the information they need to make informed investment decisions. Part of the division's responsibility is to interpret the laws—starting with the 1933 act, but including all subsequent disclosure legislation—and develop regulations congruous with all of this legislation. Furthermore, the division is charged with the task of keeping tabs on the accounting profession, focusing primarily on the Financial Accounting Standards Board (FASB), a body whose efforts have resulted in the creation of "generally accepted accounting principles," or GAAP.

The Division of Market Regulation is responsible for creating and upholding standards of integrity and efficiency for the markets. It closely regulates the key players in the operation of the markets, including broker-dealers, stock exchanges (SROs), clearing agencies, transfer agents, the National Association of Securities Dealers (NASD), securities information processors, and the Securities Investor Protection Corporation (SIPC). Some of the division's regulatory functions include performing market surveillance, implementing the SEC's solvency requirements for broker-dealers, creating and interpreting rules for operating the securities markets, and reviewing any proposal for new rules (or amendments to existing rules) brought forth by the SROs.

The SEC's third structural division is the Division of Investment Management. As its name suggests, its purpose is to regulate the $15-trillion investment management industry. This division administrates the laws applicable to investment companies, mutual funds, and investment advisers; it interprets securities laws in cases involving investment companies or investment advisers. Finally, the division regulates public-utility holding companies, a task that is of increasing importance, given the deregulation of the utilities industries.

The last of the four divisions, the Division of Enforcement, investigates potential violations of securities laws. When a possible violation is brought to the division's attention, the division makes a recommendation to the SEC that the commission bring either a civil action (heard in federal court) or an administrative action (heard by an independent administrative law judge) against the alleged perpetrator. The Division of Enforcement works closely with the other three divisions to root out those who breach securities legislation. It gathers evidence from many sources, including investor complaints, the SEC's high-tech surveillance systems, press reports and news items, and information provided by SROs, such as the NASD.

The SEC only possesses civil enforcement authority—that is, it cannot act in criminal matters. It does, however, work diligently with various local and federal law-enforcement agencies, providing them with detailed information relevant to criminal investigations. When necessary, the SEC calls in the big guns— the Department of Justice, the U.S. Attorney's Office, and the FBI. All three organizations have the authority to arrest and lay charges against perpetrators of securities crimes such as fraud, money laundering, and racketeering.

One of the SROs that works most effectively with the SEC is the National Association of Securities Dealers. The NASD was established in 1938 in accordance with the Maloney Act, an amendment to the Securities Act of 1934. A nonprofit, self-regulating body, the NASD is sponsored and overseen by the SEC. Its mandate is "to bring integrity to the markets and confidence to investors." The association saves taxpayers a tremendous amount of money by shouldering much of the burden of regulating the OTC markets, including the NASDAQ. From wire houses to boiler rooms, any firm dealing in OTC securities must register with the association, as must any broker or dealer involved in OTC securities. Because so many companies are traded over the counter these days, almost all brokerages are registered with the NASD. Its membership includes over 5,500 brokerage houses, the more than 92,000 branch offices of these houses, and over 675,000 securities professionals. These numbers alone give us a sense of the tremendous size and scope of the activities of the NASD and the OTC market.

Most established members of the investment community understand the importance of the NASD and are proud to belong to the association. They know that the survival of the markets and of the businesses they encompass depends upon a strong, well-supported NASD. The activities of the NASD include the following: registering members; writing the rules and setting the standards that keep the industry ethical and relevant; educating private investors and professionals; reviewing sales literature and advertisements for accuracy and appropriate level of disclosure; operating the world's largest securities dispute resolution forum (offering both arbitration and mediation services); providing the public with employment and disciplinary histories for all its members; and monitoring the OTC markets to ensure that all of its members are complying with the applicable rules and standards.

The NASD is organized into three primary divisions: Regulatory Policy and Oversight, Regulatory Services and Operations, and Dispute Resolution. Although all three divisions work together to realize the mission of the NASD, Regulatory Services and Operations houses the body that is most directly concerned with boiler room–style manipulations: the Department of Market Regulation. The department is responsible for monitoring the OTC markets and for identifying questionable practices and activities.

The department itself is divided into three specialized teams of skilled and experienced investigators: a team to investigate insider trading, a team to handle short-sale situations, and a team to detect fraud. Among the resources team members draw upon are customer complaints (the NASD receives over 5,000 per year), anonymous tips, and a series of impressive high-tech tools capable of locating and confirming illegal market activity.

The NASD uses three computerized systems to detect illicit activity. One is called INSITE, and it employs a highly analytical engine to recognize patterns and to mine data on brokerages presenting the greatest threat to market integrity. Then there is a similar system, called ADS—Advanced Detection System— which monitors trading and isolates questionable activity. The final point in the NASD's technological trident is SONAR software, a proprietary program that cross-analyzes trades, news announcements (including Internet news postings and chats), SEC filings, and information gathered from the other systems (such as volume concentration, volume and price spikes, and quote sequences).

If an NASD member's activity violates the rules, then the association has recourse to a range of disciplinary actions. It may opt to levy steep fines or even expel the offending member from the industry. Such expulsions can be temporary or permanent; in the latter situation, the member is barred from participating in the OTC markets for life. If the NASD determines that not only are there violations of its own regulations but also violations of the law, then it will ask the SEC to evaluate the matter as well. In some cases, the Department of Justice will enter the picture and further prosecution and punishment will ensue.

The NASD takes its enforcement responsibilities very seriously, fully aware that without the threat of punitive repercussions, the unethical and criminal elements of the investment world would gravely compromise market integrity. Many brokers, dealers, and market makers are frustrated at having to comply with the NASD's rules because it's a time-consuming daily chore. But clearly those rules lend crucial support to the NASD's mission of sustaining a reliable market system and maintaining investor confidence.

9

Be Careful What You Wish For

EXPOSÉ

It was mid-November. Another bone-chilling Chicago winter was setting in. Mike Stokes sat by the window of his Wacker Street office, looking down at the bustling sidewalk and thinking hard about the conversation he'd just had with his cousin Terry in California. Terry Randall had left the Windy City for L.A. three years earlier, and, being a go-getter like Stokes, she'd found a job right away as a sales assistant in a brokerage called Goldberg and Stevens Financial. Within a year, she'd passed all of her licensing exams; within two years, she'd passed her Series 24 exam and been promoted to office manager.

In the same three-year interval, Stokes had built up his graphic design and printing business from a two-man, one-room operation to a going concern with seven employees. He was making great money—over $100,000 a year—but he felt dissatisfied. He craved excitement, and his life wasn't offering it to him.

His partner, Bob Jameson, loved the business, and Stokes had seriously contemplated selling him his stake. The impulse to sell was reawakened by his cousin's phone call. Terry had told him all about Goldberg and Stevens. The firm's top broker was pulling in over $600,000 annually and working just four hours a day. Stokes himself was only making a fraction of that, and he was putting in 12-hour days. And there were other success stories in Cousin Terry's firm. Goldberg and Stevens employed 10 brokers, and the lowest guy on the ladder was pulling in $6,000 a month. He'd only been working there a year.

Stokes turned his attention to his computer screen, where a newsletter layout was displayed, but he couldn't focus. He shut down the computer, shaking his head. Sure, he was successful in his own right, and he was his own boss—a very important consideration. But he was bored. Twelve hours a day of graphic design was pure tedium. He was also fed up with Chicago's frigid winters and the icy winds howling in off the lake. He couldn't help it—he longed for California, palm tree paradise. But giving up everything he'd labored so hard to create? Breaking it to his family, who were all so proud of what he'd accomplished? The prospect was daunting.

Pushing his chair away from his desk, Stokes emitted a loud sigh. He took his coat from the hook and went into the large room where his team of graphic artists tapped busily at their computer keys. Bob Jameson was visible through the window overlooking the press room, happily feeding paper into a humming machine. Resisting the impulse to tell his partner where his thoughts were leading, Stokes asked the bespectacled, middle-aged receptionist to tell anyone who might be looking for him that he'd gone home early. He needed more time to think.

The elevator doors opened on the lobby, and Stokes strolled out, exiting the building through double-paned glass doors. He picked up a steaming espresso at the Italian coffee shop on the corner and headed for the steps leading down to the "L." Riding the train, he was lost in a daydream featuring sunshine, beaches, and bikini-clad blonds.

By the time he got home, he had come to his senses and was starting to mull over the numbers involved in selling his share of the company to Jameson. For the rest of the afternoon, he sat at his home computer composing an offer to sell. They owned almost all of the shop's fixed assets free and clear; and his portion of the accounts receivable should total nearly $300,000—more than enough for him to live on while he got himself up and running in a new locale. Looking at this figure on the screen before him, Stokes had to chuckle. It seemed a paltry sum when you considered that the broker Terry had told him about earned that much every six months.

Bright and early the next morning, Stokes caught the "L." He wanted to get to the office before Jameson did and collect his thoughts. Not that he had any doubts about his decision to sell. One way or another, he was going to divest himself of the graphic arts shop and move to Los Angeles.

Jameson sat quietly as Stokes laid out his proposal and the timeline for the sale, his face reflecting his surprise. Stokes finished up and asked him what he thought of it all. Flipping through the document his partner had provided for him, Jameson answered, "I think you need to do what is right for you, Mike." The two agreed to get their attorneys working on the sale and the dissolution of the partnership, and Stokes promised to finish up the jobs he was in charge of.

Things moved more quickly than they had expected, and the sale was finalized by mid-December. For Stokes, it was like being caught up in a whirlwind, and before he knew it he was ringing in 1994 on an L.A. hotel rooftop with Terry and several of her Goldberg and Stevens colleagues. Stokes was soon to become the newest member of the Goldberg and Stevens team. It was all very nerve-wracking and exhilarating.

In his own company, Stokes had acted as the primary sales force, but the experience he'd gained from this didn't help him much when it came to brokerage sales. During his first six weeks at Goldberg and Stevens, he received a remarkable education in verbal manipulation. Stokes had always been under the impression that to do well in business, you had to display a certain professionalism. He truly believed that "the customer is always right" and that a solid business must be founded on respect for the client. But Brad Michaels, the firm's sales manager, turned his head around.

Michaels was unlike anyone Stokes had ever met. He was also unlike anyone Stokes expected to find working in what he considered—at least at first—a conservative place of business. Initially, Michaels appeared normal enough. He was of average height, dark-haired, clean-cut, with an athletic build. His wife, Cindy, seemed regular too—an attractive brunette with a salon tan. But Stokes started to notice that Cindy came to Goldberg and Stevens quite often, and she'd announce to anyone within earshot on her way into her husband's office that she was there for a "nooner."

This alone struck Stokes as odd behavior for the workplace, but it didn't stop there. A couple of times, Cindy would be accompanied by another attractive woman when she came for a closed-door session in Brad's office. Later, Stokes learned that Brad and Cindy Michaels were swingers. They swapped and shared sexual partners, and they were quite open about it. But no one raised an eyebrow at Goldberg and Stevens. Everyone at the firm seemed to have a personal recipe for deviance.

On the top of the heap was Rick Wright, the firm's owner. His employees worshipped the ground he walked on—after all, every single broker in the firm had Wright to thank for his or her success. Wright was a master of motivation. Every Monday morning, he called the entire crew into his office for a sales meeting, during which he would impart to them the "sacred pitches." Wright liked to refine and develop the pitch not only to accommodate whatever deals were on the table, but also to keep things interesting for his brokers. He'd present the new deals, then he'd present their respective pitches, and then he'd wind up the meeting on an exuberant note. Stokes couldn't get over it. The brokers would go streaming out of Wright's office and start calling their clients immediately. They'd all deliver the pitches Wright had given them verbatim.

Wright also used the most powerful motivator of them all—cash—to pump up his crew. He paid them on a per-deal basis, and this made them very happy. As soon as a broker closed a client on the phone, he'd tell that client he was switching the call over to accounting so he or she could make payment arrangements. Terry Randall, as office manager, would then pick up the line and take the client's contact information, adding that a courier would be dispatched to pick up the check that afternoon. Her next step was to call FedEx. A few hours later, Wright would call FedEx, and upon confirmation of the pickup he'd write a check to the broker who'd made the sale. His cash-happy crew loved this setup, mainly because they tended to spend their money as fast, if not faster, than they earned it. Such was the culture of the industry. These people lived large—they went at it like they had a million bucks in the bank, but they were really just existing from one sale to the next. They were all caught up in the feeling that it would last forever.

And Rick Wright was no different. He owned a house in Beverly Hills and drove a convertible Bentley. He only ate restaurant food, and he only dined at the best establishments. His suits were custom made, and his watches cost more than his suits. His lifestyle requirements frequently put a strain on his wallet, and when he was in a pinch he'd bring in articles from home—sculptures, vases, paintings, clothing—and sell them to anyone at the firm who was interested for a fraction of their value. Out of this arrangement Wright got a temporary reprieve from his creditors and his brokers got some bargain-priced souvenirs of their boiler-room days.

All of this was a far cry from what Stokes was used to in terms of workplace behavior and personal financial management. His habits had always been conservative, even frugal— he'd been brought up that way. Strangely, however, the profligacy he was witnessing didn't repel him—he was intrigued. This new approach to fun awakened the sleeping rebel in him. He wanted to join the party.

The top guy Cousin Terry had told him about—the one who pulled in $600,000 a year—was named Bill Lynch, but everyone just called him Billy. Lynch could sell refrigerators to Eskimos, and his ego was even bigger than the oceanfront Santa Monica mansion he inhabited with his girlfriend, Amanda. A recovering alcoholic, Lynch claimed to have kicked the habit by finding God in cocaine. There was some animosity between

Lynch and Michaels. Office lore had it that a year earlier, the two had agreed to swap their women, Cindy and Amanda, but Amanda had balked, refusing to even kiss Brad Michaels. The well-seasoned Cindy, however, had no problem screwing Billy Lynch's brains out. The fallout had prompted the creation of an unwritten ban on office affairs (if this "affair" could be said to fall into that category).

The guy with the second-highest annual income at Goldberg and Stevens was Noah Stein. He had a house in Malibu, and his wife, Lois, owned her own beauty spa. By nature a quiet man, Stein kept himself apart from the office dramas and excesses. This was not to say, however, that Stein was some kind of model of the professional broker. As Stokes came to realize, Stein had a knack for setting up deals, but he was pulling the same manipulations as everyone else—he just didn't make a spectacle of himself while doing it. Stein was such a consummate liar that he even seemed to have convinced himself of his own authenticity.

The wildest of the Goldberg and Stevens bunch had to be Anthony Cruz. Though he wasn't as prosperous as the rest, he partied the hardest. He had a certain talent as a salesman, but he didn't advance in his career because his only goal was to make enough money to keep the party going. One essential party ingredient for Cruz was heroin. He had an overpowering addiction, which Wright's payment-upon-sale approach accommodated perfectly. Cruz would show up for work when he needed a fix or party money—maybe two days a week—and work hard to make a sale. Then he'd collect his check, and no one would see him again until the money ran out.

Then there was David Stanley, the most personable of the Goldberg and Stevens crew. He and Stokes became fast friends. Stanley and Cruz both lived in the Orchid Arms Hotel; Stein had also lived there until he met Lois. The establishment suited the lifestyles of these fast-lane brokers. Their weekly rent was only $300, and the semi-rundown old haunt was located in the decadent heart of Hollywood. Both Cruz and Stanley had already resided at the Orchid for three years when Stokes arrived in L.A. It wasn't long before he joined them there. His plan was to stay for a week or two—just until Jameson's payments started coming through. Terry Randall had offered to put him up, but he didn't want to impose—she'd done enough for him already.

Stokes's room at the Orchid, on the second floor of the three-story building, was spacious but dark. Its stale, musty smell inspired him—it made him think of all the aspiring young actors and actresses who had occupied the premises over the years—and it creeped him out at the same time. The first nights he spent there were restless ones. A low-flying police helicopter woke him at 2:00 one morning, its brilliant searchlight sweeping the room. The thing was like a giant mechanical insect from some B-movie intent on devouring its prey. Stokes couldn't wait for Jameson to send him some cash.

His first day at Goldberg and Stevens was illuminating, to say the least. First of all, he discovered that the place was as smoky as the pubs he used to frequent back in Chicago. Everyone at the firm was a chain-smoker, and they lit up every chance they got, in defiance of city ordinances. Also, everybody drank at work, stocking their drawers with their favorite tipple.

Another interesting aspect of the place was that everyone used a pseudonym. The reason for this, Terry explained, was that it provided the firm with a way to deflect a disgruntled client bent on getting a scoundrel broker fired—Wright could claim to have fired the culprit while merely retiring the pseudonym.

All of this seemed over the top to Stokes, but he just laughed it off. He was committed to making it out here on the West Coast, and if this is what the workplace scene consisted of, he could handle it—no big deal. Besides, Wright and Michaels—management—didn't care what their brokers were up to as long as they kept on closing deals.

Goldberg and Stevens brokers sold all kinds of things: antique coins; autographs of sports and entertainment figures; IPOs for Internet startups; and—most lucrative of all—shares in limited partnerships (LPs) for oil, cable, and wireless. The markup on the memorabilia was big—upwards of 20 to 30 percent, but the LPs could be filed for a hundred bucks per contract and sold for as much as $7,000. Stokes was astounded at the profit that could be harvested from these contracts, and the most amazing thing was that it was all legal. That, however, was not to say it was ethical. The money raised through these LPs never went back into the businesses that issued them. It was used to pay the brokers and cover other expenses incurred during the money-raising operation; that is, the cash raised was distributed to the benefit of the brokerage. But as long as the firm did everything by the book and no broker ever promised a client that the investment would turn a profit, there was no risk of prosecution. As Wright put it, "We aren't selling investments, we're selling dreams!"

This is where Michaels came in. Besides acting as the firm's sales manager and handling most of the transactional paperwork for the deals, he tutored the brokers in the art of high-pressure sales. His brutal style of stock slinging was born from those pressure-cooker moments when you could either make the deal fly high or bring it crashing to the ground. So Michaels routinely turned up the heat on the newbies—he wanted to gauge what they were made of, and fast. There would be no mentoring or coddling here. And of course, Stokes, as the new guy, was in Michaels's sights. It was trial by fire time.

All the office phones had mouthpiece attachments that made it impossible for the person on the other end of the line to hear anything but the voice of the person speaking directly into the receiver. Michaels could stand directly behind his trainees screaming orders and obscenities at them and clients would never have a clue. The first time Michaels called Stokes a "fucking pussy," Stokes was shocked. Then the shock wore off. He soon learned that when Michaels was off the floor he was upbeat and reasonably supportive, and on the floor he was downright abusive. Michaels sent many aspirants packing their first day on the job, and if Stokes hadn't been Terry Randall's cousin, the same fate would likely have befallen him. At first, Stokes was clumsy— barely able to stammer out the pitch, backing down when faced with an aggressive prospect. "You're going to let her do that to you?!" Michaels would shout. "You can't let the client close you! You just got shut out by an old fucking lady, Stokes! How does that make you feel, you big pussy?"

To arm himself for his battle for survival at Goldberg and Stevens, Stokes went out and bought several books on the art of selling—in other words, on manipulating people into buying things they never knew they wanted or needed. He studied his pitches and taped them so that he could listen to his performance and refine his tone and delivery. He studied a list of typical client objections that Wright had drawn up, and he and Stanley practiced their rebuttals together.

All the while, Stokes was studying feverishly for his Series 7 licensing exam. He knew that if he didn't pass it, Michaels would can him, despite his relation to Terry. Each night, he crammed until he was exhausted; each morning, he headed back to the boiler-room cold-calling grind. The information he had to cover for the exam was voluminous, but his friends at the firm assured him that to ace the Series 7 all he had to do was commit as much of that info as he could to memory. The exam wasn't really about knowing anything; there was no thinking involved, and he'd rapidly forget everything he'd stuffed into his head anyway. It was just a game they all had to play—and win. His friends advised him to keep the whole thing in perspective: he wasn't studying to become a financial professional, he was studying to get his license to sell.

The environment at the Orchid Arms turned out to be ideal for someone in Stokes's immediate situation. The shabbiness of his surroundings made him strive even harder for his ticket to a better life, and living in the same building as Stanley and Cruz meant having ready access to help with his studies and companionship when he needed to blow off a little steam. The two brokers became his pack, and he ran with them. Cruz went out every night, and he was always happy to have Stokes join him in his revels. Stanley was generally more disciplined and focused on making a success of himself, but he did have a drinking problem, and on a number of occasions he really tied one on. More than once, Stokes had found him passed out on the sidewalk in front of the Orchid, still clutching a vodka bottle.

As determined as he was to establish himself in a new career, Stokes hadn't forgotten that one of the reasons he'd ditched his setup in Chicago was that he was looking for more excitement in life. Hanging with Cruz and Stanley, therefore, fit in with his plans. Cruz was a live heavy-metal aficionado, and he knew all the best rock clubs in town. One night, after guzzling a few beers in Cruz's room, Stokes, Stanley, and Cruz took a cab to Silver Lake, to a club called The Garage. Cruz wanted to catch a band that was playing there—one of his friends was in it.

The place was small and dark. The crowd was an eclectic mix of punkers, Goths, and metal heads. Stokes and Stanley were obvious outsiders, but somehow Cruz fit right in. The trio sat at a table with a bunch of Cruz's rowdy acquaintances. By this time, Jameson had started paying Stokes, so he had plenty of cash on him. He found himself buying round after round for the table, making himself very popular in the process. He also found himself becoming very drunk. The band was oppressively loud, and not really to Stokes's taste, but the entire scene was exactly what he'd been looking for—it was a crazy slice of life, and he never would have experienced it in Chicago. When Cruz's cohorts invited the brokers to a house party, Stokes was all for it.

They drove in a caravan from Silver Lake to Hollywood. After following Sunset for a while, they turned onto a winding canyon road. They finally pulled up in front of a house in the hills between Hollywood and the Valley. Several members of the gang from the bar shared the rent on the place. It was quite remote—Stokes had no idea that such places existed in L.A. It felt mysterious and exciting to be there.

The house was large and old, but it was sparsely furnished. A pair of couches, a coffee table, a marble bar, and an entertainment center did little to fill the cavernous living room. There were already quite a few people milling around when the three brokers entered. The stereo was blaring the kind of music they'd heard at the club, and the partyers bore a strong resemblance to the clubbers. In the big, florescent-lit kitchen, a keg of beer had been installed, and the three wasted no time in filling their plastic cups to the brim. A short while later, when Stokes was helping himself to a third cup of brew, he was greeted by a blond wearing strange green eye shadow. She introduced herself and told him that she'd seen him at the club. Laughing, she mentioned that he had really stood out in that crowd. Stokes accepted her teasing with good humor and thought to himself that this might be a good occasion to try out a little of that salesman charm he'd been working so hard to develop.

So he chatted with the girl awhile, and when he moved in confidently for the kiss, she didn't object in the least. This kind of bravado was unprecedented for Stokes. While he was no slouch with the ladies, he had always been more comfortable with the gentlemanly approach than the cocky bad-boy one. But since he'd landed in California, he'd noticed a shift in his personality. Now he engaged everyone he met in conversation, because every encounter—social or professional—was an opportunity to sell. He'd quickly learned that an effective salesman sells himself, not just a product. Early on, Wright had imparted a piece of wisdom that he'd taken to heart: "People do business with people they like." Still, Stokes knew that there was more to it than that, and as he developed as a salesman he also kept in mind that the best salespeople apply their craft with such subtlety that their prospects don't even know they're being led into the close.

Stokes's interaction with the flirty blond didn't end with a chat and a kiss. After the kiss, she led him to a makeshift office outfitted with a computer, a desk, and a chair. Closing and locking the door behind her, she explained to Stokes that she was good friends with one of the guys who lived in the house—not to worry. He was so drunk by this time that the only thing he was worried about was whether he had a rubber in his wallet. As he fumbled through his billfold in search of protection, the girl stripped down to her bra and panties. Stokes was becoming frantic—he was rubberless! Thinking fast, he decided that Cruz, the preeminent ladies man, would have a supply. With a kiss, he excused himself and began to hunt for his savior.

He scoured the house, moving from room to room and asking everyone he met if they'd seen Cruz. Finally, someone directed him to a small upstairs loft. He knocked. There was no answer, so he opened the door and poked his head inside. Big, soft cushions were scattered on the floor, and strands of Christmas lights adorned the walls. A ceiling fixture with a purple bulb provided most of the illumination, and in its psychedelic glow Stokes saw three shadowy reclining figures. As his eyes became accustomed to the dim light, Stokes recognized Cruz; the small room's other two occupants were women, and they lay on either side of Cruz. Their eyes were closed, and they had peaceful expressions on their faces.

Stokes called to Cruz several times before he answered. "Mikey. What's up?" came the slow, affectionate response. When Stokes asked if he had a spare condom, Cruz said, "No, man, but I've got something better. You ever tried H?" Stokes asked him what he was talking about. Cruz gave a languorous laugh and said, "Heroin." While Stokes had partaken of marijuana, LSD, and cocaine, he'd never even considered doing anything as hard as heroin. And no way was he going to touch the stuff now. He was strangely affected by Cruz's revelation that he was into "H."

He shut the door and made his way back to the office. The girl was gone. It was now 3:30 in the morning, and he'd left her alone for too long. He decided to crash right where he was, so he set his watch alarm for 6:00 a.m.—he had to be at his desk at Goldberg and Stevens at 6:30—curled up on the floor, and nodded off.

When the alarm beeped, Stokes sat bolt upright and tried to orient himself. He felt horrible. As he jammed his feet into his shoes, his head swam and pounded. He was sweating profusely. Staggering over to the phone on the desk, he dialed the number of a cab company whose business card he found in his wallet. Before his call connected, however, he realized that he had no idea where he was. He slammed down the receiver and headed off to find someone who could tell him. Entering the large front room, he spotted David Stanley huddled in a corner, sound asleep. Stokes picked his way across the floor, stepping over slumbering bodies, and reached his friend. It was hard to wake him. When he finally managed it, he told Stanley that they only had 15 minutes to get to work. But Stanley didn't care. He'd been at the firm long enough that Michaels no longer kept watch over his comings and goings. Stokes, on the other hand, was a new guy, and he had good reason to worry about being late—Michaels could fire him in a second. He finally persuaded Stanley, who had partied at the house on several occasions, to help him get out of the hills and back to town.

By the time the taxi arrived, Stokes was already 10 minutes late for work. When he finally dragged himself through the office door, it was 7:00. He thanked his lucky stars that Michaels wasn't on the floor, and his office door was shut. But Noah Stein was there, diligently working the pitch for an LP Wright had put together.

Sliding into the chair behind his desk, Stokes felt close to vomiting. He stared blankly at the phone for a few minutes, and then he remembered that there was a coffeemaker in the lunchroom. Making his way through the largely deserted front office, he noticed that Terry wasn't at her desk. He assumed she was meeting with Michaels—he hoped not about him. He wondered briefly why the trainee who had been working the phones the day before wasn't in yet. Maybe he'd already quit or been fired. Stokes couldn't wait until he'd achieved the level of production that would allow him to make his own hours and not be chained to his desk.

The pot was already full of steaming coffee. Stokes gratefully filled a large styrofoam cup, added nondairy creamer and a big splash of water from the water cooler, and started sipping. Before long, the fluid and the caffeine had done their work, making him feel like he just might make it through the day. Back at his desk, he shuffled through his lead cards and prepared to start making calls. He was startled to hear Stein's voice behind him: "Michaels is gone." Turning to look up at his colleague, Stokes said, "Huh?"

"He's gone. Rick and Terry are in there going through his shit right now."

"What happened?"

"I don't know yet. I just know he didn't come in this morning, and Terry said he wasn't coming in at all. She said she'd explain later."

Relief that he wouldn't be subjected to the notorious Michaels third degree while suffering from one of the worst hangovers he'd had in years flooded through Stokes. Then, by turns, he felt astonished and curious. It was another half hour before the door to Michaels's office opened and Rick Wright emerged, followed by Terry Randall. They were both carrying large boxes. Terry greeted her cousin as she passed his desk.

She went into Wright's office, dropped her box on the floor, and went to her own desk.

Once Wright had closed his door, she came over to talk to Stokes. She pulled a chair up close to where he sat and began speaking in an undertone. Michaels, she said, had been doctoring his records to skim money from markups on house products. Wright had been suspicious for a few months now, and he'd started keeping a set of mirror records in order to catch his sales manager red-handed. When he thought that he'd collected enough evidence, he'd confronted Michaels and threatened him with criminal and civil action. Michaels had retorted that he knew everything that went on in this office, and he had plenty of dirt to present to the authorities himself. This tactic failed to intimidate Wright, who ordered Michaels to pack up and leave immediately. Then he'd escorted Michaels from the building. It all sounded pretty intense.

Terry went on to tell Stokes that the new trainee had been fired. In fact, she'd canned him herself. The day before, the trainee had been working late in the afternoon, forbidden to leave until he'd come up with at least 15 leads for the day—the usual trainee treatment. All the brokers had left by 4:00, and Terry was the only other person there. Feeling hungry, she stepped out to buy a burrito, but when she was halfway to the taco stand, she realized that she had no money on her. She turned around and went back to the office to get the change purse she'd left in her desk.

Bursting through the door, she strode over to her desk. Then, out of the corner of her eye, she saw the trainee scrambling to— pull up his pants? That's right. She stared in amazement as the blushing young man struggled to pull himself together. He still had the phone receiver pinned between shoulder and ear, and he was talking to a client. It dawned on Terry that the trainee had been masturbating under his desk while he was making his calls. She couldn't believe it. Stammering, she ordered him to get out and never come back. Despite his hangover, Stokes laughed hard at her story.

Stanley didn't show up for work until the next morning. And it would be quite awhile before Stokes laid eyes on Cruz again, either at work or at the Orchid. The night in the hills—Cruz's revelation of his heroin addiction and his own wicked hangover—had somewhat dampened Stokes's initial enthusiasm for the wild West Coast lifestyle. He decided to buckle down and focus on achieving professional success. Admittedly, he was always up for a good time, but he no longer wanted to go at it like some 20-year-old kid. He wanted to enjoy his downtime the way he imagined Wright and Lynch did—hosting sophisticated house parties, cruising aboard their yachts, flying out to Vegas to stay in private bungalows and throw around more cash than the Corleones.

Stokes also resolved to learn as much as he could from Lynch. This wouldn't be easy. Lynch didn't have much interest in tutoring novices. Furthermore, he wasn't exactly putting in long hours at work, and the only way Stokes could gain access to him was to go into his office with a trumped-up question and eavesdrop while he waited for the broker to get off the phone. Still, he did it. He listened carefully to everything Lynch said, and he watched what he did. He picked up Lynch's calm, confident delivery and noted the catchphrases he tended to use.

Soon enough, Stokes was feeling stronger and more knowledgeable while working his pitches. He was opening more accounts. Plus, he was learning to second trade his clients. His favorite tactic was to pull them in on a "private placement," get his hands on their money, and then sell them on a "faster-moving momentum play." It sounded good, and most clients bit. He also enjoyed pitching IPOs—in the mid-1990s bull market, you could sell people on the next big thing, usually tech or biotech, without breaking a sweat. With each call, Stokes refined his sales technique until he'd finally outstripped both Stanley and Cruz. Next, he set his sights on besting Stein, who was bringing in about 20 large per month. Stokes had climbed to about 14. He was moving up faster than any new broker Wright had ever seen.

Jameson's installments were still coming in, and this money, combined with his fat broker's commissions, afforded Stokes an impressive lifestyle. He was now a familiar face at L.A.'s best restaurants, and he hung out in swank clubs almost every night. Stanley and Cruz still had a fondness for the Orchid, but Stokes had come to detest the place. He signed a lease on a comfortable bachelor pad just north of Santa Monica and bought a convertible Mercedes.

And the deals kept rolling in. Wright was setting up all sorts of lucrative ventures, including some underwritings that put both cash and stock into their accounts. Stokes kept up his quest to become the best salesman around, and in this fast and furious market, most of his colleagues felt driven to step up their efforts as well. Soon, Goldberg and Stevens was being referred to as the hottest boutique brokerage in the city, and its brokers had earned the reputation of being true ballers.

In the two years Stokes had been with the firm, he had transformed himself into a high-powered broker. He was already earning $25,000 a month, and as he looked ahead to the future, he saw himself rising even higher. Of course, it's at times like these, when you scan the horizon and see nothing but clear sailing ahead, that a storm blows up out of nowhere.

In retrospect, Stokes identified the firing of Michaels as the beginning of the end of Goldberg and Stevens. Michaels had been true to his word when he told Wright he'd take his insider dirt to the authorities. One Monday morning, Stokes arrived at the office to find FBI agents interrogating his boss. No one had any doubt about who had tipped them off.

At first, Stokes was sure that they were all going to go down for some deal Wright had put together without telling them it was illegal, but he was wrong. Stein filled him in. Wright, he explained, was being forced to surrender records related to some Cayman Islands accounts he held. Although Wright hadn't actually been charged with anything, he had ignored a court order to produce the records. To Stokes, this screamed tax evasion. And Stein added that there was a possibility money laundering charges would be laid—the fact that the FBI was involved and that offshore account holders frequently committed this offence seemed to suggest it.

In the few weeks that spanned the FBI's visit and Wright's arrest, Stokes's world crumbled around him. As his earning power had increased, his friendship with Billy Lynch, the firm's top broker, had intensified, and Lynch was a hardcore cocaine addict. The man never seemed to sleep. When he'd moved on to crystal meth, he'd introduced Stokes to the stuff. At first, Stokes found it too intense—it kept him awake for up to three days at a time—but he soon learned to regulate his dosage. He came to love the energy the crystal meth high infused him with.

Before long, meth was Stokes's morning coffee—a quick line in the morning kept him going. He never became a volume user, but he grew to rely on meth as a tool for sustaining his success. His alcohol consumption increased as well, and he had plenty of drinking buddies—all of the firm's brokers were alcoholics. But he kept his drug use under wraps.

A few days before Wright was arrested, something terrible happened. Cruz had disappeared again, and the manager of the Orchid stopped Stokes and Stanley on their way to Stanley's room to prepare for a night on the town. He told them that Cruz hadn't paid his rent that week. If he didn't show up soon, the manager warned, he was going to chuck his belongings into the street. Stanley paid the $300, and the manager calmed down, but Stokes had a bad feeling about the whole thing. Cruz had vanished many times before, playing hooky from work, but he'd always returned to his room at fairly regular intervals to shower and change or have a tryst with one of his ladies before taking off again. This time, however, Stokes and Stanley hadn't seen their friend in more than 10 days.

Two days later, Stokes picked up Stanley and they drove to work together. They found two police cars and an ambulance pulled up in front of the building. Terry Randall was standing alone on the sidewalk, crying. Wright and Stein hadn't shown up yet. Gradually, Stokes and Stanley extracted the story from the devastated Terry. Cruz had broken into the office late the night before, and, leaning against the wall near his desk, he'd shot up. Terry had arrived at work early, and she'd been the one to find Cruz, dead from an apparent heroin overdose. Stokes was devastated too, but he wasn't really surprised—it had only been a matter of time before the hard-living broker went too far.

Shortly afterwards, Stokes was at home in a meth-induced delirium when Terry called to tell him that Wright was about to be charged with fraud, money laundering, and tax evasion. She reassured him that he, himself, had nothing to worry about—the authorities knew that he hadn't been party to anything illegal. But Stokes was worried. He stared at his haggard, stoned face in the bathroom mirror and it all hit him—the firm was finished, Cruz was dead, and he was in desperate need of help. He was very fortunate to have a healthy bank account, because it wouldn't be replenished for some time. Acting fast, before he could change his mind, he called a rehabilitation center he'd heard about and booked himself in.

For two months, Stokes battled to get his body and mind back on track, and he emerged from the center with a new sense of himself. He began attending AA and NA meetings; he also went to services at a local church, where he found strength in religion—so much so that he became a born-again Christian. He realized that although he had to break free of the self-destructive lifestyle he'd embraced in his naïve pursuit of excitement, he didn't have to abandon his profession or his goal of living well.

For the first time, the world of the big, established financial institutions beckoned to Stokes. Those who plied their trade in the boutique brokerages tended to dismiss the wire houses—such as Morgan Stanley, Merrill Lynch, or Solomon Smith Barney—as bastions of the wimpy broker. The conventional wisdom in certain circles was that only those who couldn't hack it in the trenches where the real money was to be found would consider working in such places. Real brokers went the boutique route. But in his rejuvenated state, Stokes felt drawn to the stability that a wire house career offered. The wire house air of legitimacy also held a powerful appeal for him. He was worldly enough to know that established financial institutions had their own problems and their fair share of bullshit, but after what he'd been through, he could handle all of that with ease.

So Stokes cracked open the phone book and started calling sales managers at every branch office in L.A. Most were reluctant to hire a former chop shopper, but he did find a couple of managers willing to talk to him. He was candid about his personal and professional history, and, as luck would have it, he finally encountered a sales manager whose experiences paralleled his own. The man was willing to give Stokes a chance, and he took it gratefully.

The drive and determination that had once propelled him to the top of the Goldberg and Stevens heap kicked in once again, and within a few years Stokes was the most successful broker in the region. He won several sales awards and became sales manager of a branch office. Stokes remained sober and motivated, and what helped him to stay the course was the hard lessons he'd learned during his time in the boiler room.

A Context for Corruption

The ins and outs of many illegal business activities—like insider trading, misrepresentation, and falsified operational filings—are fairly easy for most people to understand. But it's not enough simply to be aware of such practices. Every investor should possess an understanding of the broad context of scams and market manipulations. A general understanding of the markets can protect investors against those who attempt to corrupt the system.

For most people, the term "stock market" evokes images of the frenetic trading floor of the New York Stock Exchange (NYSE) or NASDAQ's electronic ticker. But in the United States, there are a number of exchanges where securities are traded in their simplest forms: stocks, bonds, subscription rights and warrants, stock and index options, and basic derivative products. Each of these exchanges is a "self-regulating organization," or SRO, and each maintains its own set of rules designed to support and enhance federal securities legislation.

These SROs are: the NYSE, the NASDAQ Stock Market, the American Stock Exchange (AMEX, located in New York), the Boston Stock Exchange, the Midwest Stock Exchange (in Chicago), the Pacific Stock Exchange (in Los Angeles and San Francisco), the Philadelphia Stock Exchange (in Philadelphia and Miami), the Intermountain Exchange (in Salt Lake City), and the Spokane and Cincinnati Exchanges. Stock exchanges headquartered outside of New York City are considered regional exchanges, but they may list securities that are listed on the NYSE and the AMEX. All exchanges are linked via computer by means of the Intermarket Trading System (ITS), and all fall under the regulatory jurisdiction of a federal entity called the Securities and Exchange Commission (SEC).

Any company that lists its securities on these exchanges must register its initial public offering (IPO) or any secondary offering with the SEC—thus the term "registered securities." It is illegal to sell an unregistered security on the open market. However, a company, or issuer, may sell unregistered offerings directly to an investor if it obtains a letter of intent signed by that investor; the letter must stipulate that the purchase of the security is for investment purposes only.

All of the U.S. exchanges, except for NASDAQ, work on a floor-trading system, which involves designating a specialist for each listed security. A specialist may represent more than one security, and he or she must meet minimum capital requirements established by the SEC. The responsibility of the specialist is to maintain an efficient market and to strike a balance between the supply of a given security and the demand for it. The specialist is also required to keep a record of all transactions.

Regulations prohibit the specialist from acting ahead of

orders placed—that is, the specialist cannot execute a new trade before all previous orders for that security are executed. Specialists are assigned to specific trading posts on the floor of the exchange. When you see footage of the NYSE trading floor on television, you can pick out the specialists: they are the people being mobbed by frantic floor brokers trying to get their orders placed as quickly as possible.

Of all the exchanges, the NASDAQ is the only one that doesn't use specialists in its operations. Instead, it employs the "over the counter" (OTC) system, a network of computer and telephone connections that links dealers and market makers. In the OTC markets, the dealer plays a key role in shepherding a security from IPO to open market. The dealer is a principal, meaning that the firm the dealer works for buys and sells using its own accounts, which are called "proprietary accounts." These accounts are used to house inventories of securities.

When an investor buys a stock that a dealer holds in inventory, the transaction confirmation must record that the security came directly from the dealer's account. Stock held in a dealer's inventory and sold to the public is also known as "house stock." In a new issue or an IPO, the dealers make up the selling group responsible for distributing the offering to the public, and they are paid a concession, or commission, for their efforts.

A market maker is a dealer who maintains firm price quotes for a given OTC security. Market makers must register with the NASD, a private-sector provider of financial regulatory services that has member firms. The NASD requires a minimum of two market makers for each OTC security. This means that there are at least two dealers trading from their own accounts in any given OTC offering.

In this context, there is some room for price manipulation. Market makers can illegally drive a stock price up or down simply by bouncing the security back and forth between themselves, creating the illusion of volume. The price rises or falls depending on whether the manipulation has manufactured the signs of a stock buying spree or a stock sell-off.

Although the NASDAQ is an OTC market, it has stringent listing requirements, making it inaccessible to many newly established enterprises. Since capital markets are vital resources for emerging companies, the NASD established—in 1990, with the sanctioning of the SEC—the OTC Bulletin Board (OTC BB) to give low-net-worth companies a place to start. The listing requirements for the OTC BB are lax, permitting companies with short operating histories and minimal assets to trade. The OTC BB also lists the low-priced stocks of the smallest companies in a publication that has even lower requirements than the exchange itself. Before this publication was made available, OTC investors had to rely solely on another publication, called the Pink Sheets.

The Pink Sheets, named for the color of the paper it's printed on, is a subscription-based listing of OTC-traded companies not listed in newspapers. It not only provides bid and ask prices, but it also gives the names of the market makers. Broker-dealers put this information to a variety of uses—identifying prime targets for mergers, identifying companies that need help promoting their stock, and identifying companies that would be easy to take control of.

The realm of the OTC BB and the Pink Sheets attracts boiler-room fraudsters bent on manipulating penny stocks—that is, stocks trading for less than five dollars a share. The issuers of these stocks are usually companies in dire need of funds to support and expand their operations. Because such companies have little capitalization and net worth, they are not required to file annual reports with the SEC, which makes it very difficult for investors to research their viability. In other words, this area of the market is a shadowy place where nefarious schemes are regularly hatched and carried out.

Dealers and market makers perpetrate many of the scams in the penny-stock industry, but there are other players in the game. One such player is the trader. Simply put, a trader is someone who acts on his or her own behalf. In a brokerage, the trader is a dealer or the firm's principal, and that person must register with the NASD. In brokerages that have retail clients, traders are required to put client orders ahead of their own, and they are often responsible for stabilizing an issue that becomes unbalanced. These traders maintain firm bid and ask quotations on the securities they trade, but they pay no commissions on their trades; instead, they make their money through incremental changes in bid and ask prices—the spread.

The best-known occupation within the securities industry is that of the stockbroker. The stockbroker acts on behalf of an investor client, and he or she has a fiduciary responsibility to that client—meaning, the stockbroker is obliged by law to act in the best interests of the client. Buy or sell recommendations, financial advice of any kind, must reflect this obligation. To ensure that stockbrokers honor their fiduciary responsibilities, the exchanges have instituted regulations in which the concept of suitability is implicit. Some refer to this concept as the "know-your-customer rule," and it's based upon the risk tolerance of the client in a given transaction. The NASD's "Rules of Fair

Practice" define it as the stockbroker always having "reasonable grounds for believing" that any recommendation he or she makes is "suitable" for the client in question.

It is because they are bound by such regulations that stockbrokers making initial contact with a prospective client ask many questions about net income, net worth, investment holdings, and plans for the future. Naturally, many people find these questions invasive. But perhaps they would find them less so if they understood that the broker was merely trying to construct as complete a client profile as possible in order to avoid getting into serious trouble with the regulatory agencies.

It's ironic that this rule, made to protect investors from overzealous or unscrupulous stockbrokers, is sometimes used against brokers themselves. This is how it's done. The investor contacts a broker and asks to open an account. The broker is happy to assist. The investor provides the basic personal information, primarily a social security number, necessary to open an account. He controls the conversation, discussing with the broker a security he wishes to purchase. Suddenly, the investor announces that he has to get off the phone immediately, effectively denying the broker the opportunity to establish an adequate client profile. The investor's last words before hanging up are something like, "Just place the trade, and I'll call you back in an hour or so with the rest of my information."

The unsuspecting broker, likely a rookie, places the order. If the price of the stock goes up, the investor calls back, provides all the required information, and pays for the trade. But if the price falls, the investor refuses to pay, claiming that his suitability as an investor was not adequately determined. If pressed to pay, he threatens to turn the broker in to the authorities.

As I have mentioned, most instances of securities fraud occur in the opaque markets of the OTC BB and the Pink Sheets, with the primary instrument of deception being the penny stock. Due to the volatile and suspicious nature of penny-stock offerings, most larger firms won't even touch them. There are, however, certain brokerages that have prospered through the sale of these securities, brokerages that have often served as havens for perpetrators of fraud. These brokerages are, of course, the boiler rooms—the boutique brokerages, the chop shops, the bucket shops—that we've looked at so closely in this book.

From the mid-1980s, through the 1990s, and into the first year or so of this century, the boiler rooms had their heyday. During this era, the typical boiler-room floor—a large open area equipped with little more than desks and phones—would be packed with eager young brokers and trainees. All day long, they'd feverishly obey the command, "Pound the phones!" It was a numbers game—the more people you called, the more people you'd close.

Despite pullbacks in 1987, 1997, and 1998, the national economy surged forward, and everybody wanted to be a stockbroker. And why not? Brokers were raking it in. Guys and girls with little more than a high school education were earning tens of thousands of dollars each month, and many became overconfident wiseguys. They had attitude, and they indulged their every decadent taste and whim as soon as they got their hands on their next fat paycheck.

The average boiler room had a couple of traders, an office manager, some sales assistants, and anywhere from 3 to 300 brokers. These brokers were salespeople, pure and simple, and few had illusions about it. One joke that was often heard among boiler-room brokers during those heady market-boom years was that if you score higher than 80 percent on the licensing exam, you won't make it in the business because you know too much—your focus should always be on making the sale. "Ask for the order" was a common mantra among these brokers—you ask for the order, you listen to your prospect's objections, you refute the objections. You keep it up until your prospect either hangs up or caves in. It was high pressure all the way. And the technique worked surprisingly well when implemented by well-spoken, intelligent-sounding salespeople.

The bottom line, as I have said, is that no investment decision has to be made on the spot. As an investor, you should never succumb to high-pressure sales tactics. Research and reflection are essential. If a broker urges you to buy on the first call, then consider that behavior a red flag. Hang up the phone, or at least proceed with extreme caution. And remember that there are laws to protect the public from market scams, as well as several agencies and organizations created primarily to protect investors and maintain the credibility of the securities industry.

Sources

Bauder, Don. "Encinitas Stock Advisor Faces Charges." *San Diego Union Tribune*, 23 May 2002.

Calbreath, Dean. "From Partner to Profiteer." *San Diego Union Tribune*, 10 June 2002.

Davis, Sean, and Nicole Ridgway. "Web of Deceit: How Internet Changed Nature of Stock Fraud." Dow Jones News Service, 20 December, 1999.
www.djnewswires.com

Downes, John, and Jordan Eliot Goodman. *Dictionary of Finance and Investment Terms.* 5th ed. New York: Barron's, 1998.

Kady, Martin, II, and Eric Winig. "Reversal of Fortune." *Washington Business Journal*, 31 July 2000.

McClearn, Matthew. "Death-Spiral Finance." *Toronto Star*, 15 October 2002.

Molloy, J., and M. Fung. "Full Speed Reverse!" *Mirus Online Newsletter*, July 2001.
www.imakenews.com/rcwmirus

Mount, Ian. "Bull Market, What Hast Thou Wrought?" *Business 2.0*, August 2000.
www.business2.com

NASD Home Page.
www.nasd.com

Perlman, Jay. "Securities Fraud." *Motley Fool*, 23 February 2000.
    www.Fool.com

"The Radar Screen." *StockPatrol.com*, 12 December 2002.
    www.StockPatrol.com

Raphael, Rebecca. "Online Investment Scams." ABCNEWS.com,
    2 December 2002.
    www.ABCNEWS.com

"SEC Sues Nevada Company over Fake HIV Drug Claims." Reuters
    NewMedia, 13 August 1999.
    www.bizinfo.reuters.com

Spragins, Ellen E. "Back-Door IPOs: How to Go Public by Merging
    with a Shell Company." *Inc. Magazine*, 1 September 1989.
    www. inc.com

Taulli, Tom. "Death Spirals and Toxic Convertibles." *Internet Stock
    Report*, 18 December 2002.
    www.internetnews.com

Thevenot, Carri Geer. "Lawyer Gets Prison in Tax Fraud Scheme."
    Las Vegas Review-Journal, 9 November 2002.

U.S. Department of Justice Home Page.
    www.usdoj.gov

U.S. Securities and Exchange Commission Home Page.
    www.sec.gov